Manufacturing: New Concepts and New Technology to Meet New Competition

Edited by
James K. Brown

A Conference Report from The Conference Board

Contents

Editor's Acknowledgments

Thanks are due to:

*Evan Herbert, Project Director of the May, 1983, conference on "Meeting the New Industrial Competition," for planning the conference and enlisting the participation of the distinguished chairman and speakers on that occasion;
*Dr. Lillian W. Kay, Manager of Editorial Services for The Conference Board, and Joyce Fine Schultz, Senior Editorial Associate, for their invaluable assistance in arranging the conference materials for publication.

Some Computer and Production Terms Used in This Report

CAD: Computer-aided (or assisted) design. A process by which designs are produced and documented on a graphics video terminal controlled by a computer or microprocessor. The output of a CAD system may be conventional drawings, finished artwork for photographic reproduction. Alternatively, the output may be stored in an electrical recording for transfer to a computer-controlled machine on the shop floor.

CAM: Computer-aided (or assisted) manufacturing. A manufacturing or materials transfer process controlled by a computer program stored in the machine's electronic memory.

CIM: Computer-integrated manufacturing. An integrated production line of machining operations and intermachine materials transfer, completely controlled by computer programs. CIM may involve either one computer, or a "master computer" monitoring separate CAM systems for each machining or materials transfer station.

CNC: Computer numerical control (or computer numerically controlled) machine. In this type of CAM, the program is in the form of a list of discrete steps to be taken in sequence by the machine. The computer, in this instance, is merely an economical method of storing the programs, replacing older NC machines where storage was in such forms as punched paper tape or cards.

MRP: Stands for both manufacturing resources planning and material requirements planning. *Manufacturing resources planning* pertains to the flow of production from the purchasing of materials or parts through subsequent manufacturing stages to final assembly and test. *Material requirements planning* refers to an integrated data processing systems that begins with inputs of sales order data and sales forecasts, and breaks these down into details of parts to be ordered, parts to be manufactured, kits of parts to be assembled, and assemblies to be tested. This provides a modern form of production control.

Off line: An installation where a computer produces program information for machine or materials transfer control and places this in storage in a variety of forms for physical transfer to the controlled unit.

On line: An installation where the computer is connected directly to the machine or materials transfer unit to be controlled.

Real time: A real time computer system provides response on demand, within a fixed number of internal computer time cycles, without causing the requesting input to wait in a queue for service.

Who's Who in This Report

WILLIAM J. ABERNATHY[1]

William Barclay Harding Professor of The Management of Technology, Graduate School of Business Administration, Harvard University. As a man frequently ahead of the times, Professor Abernathy provoked controversy with his award-winning articles on "Managing Our Way to Economic Decline" (1980), and "The New Industrial Competition" (1981). His last book, *Industrial Renaissance,* coauthored with Kim B. Clark and Alan M. Kantrow, was published in April, 1983, by Basic Books. Professor Abernathy's forte was in teaching and research on the management of technology, production policy, innovation, and research and development. From 1968 to 1972, he was Assistant Professor of Business Administration, Stanford University; and from 1966 to 1968, Assistant Professor of Business Administration at the University of California at Los Angeles. From 1959 to 1961, he served as Project Manager of General Dynamics' Frankfurt Technical Office.

ROBERT J. ALLIO

President, Robert J. Allio & Associates, Inc.—a management consulting firm he founded in 1979. From 1981 to 1983, Dr. Allio served as Dean of the School of Management at Rensselaer Polytechnic Institute. Prior to 1979, he was affiliated with Arthur D. Little; and before that he was President of Canstar Communications in Toronto. From 1968 to 1975, he was Director, Corporate Planning and Development, Babcock & Wilcox. Earlier, Dr. Allio was affiliated with Westinghouse Electric Corporation. He is currently the editor and publisher of Planning Review.

JAMES E. ASHTON

Vice President and General Manager, Tulsa Division, Rockwell International Corporation. The Tulsa Division builds major elements of the B-1B Long Range Combat Aircraft, the Space Shuttle Orbiter, and the 747 Commercial Jet Liner. Before joining Rockwell, Dr. Ashton was President of Space Services, Inc. Prior to that, he was with General Dynamics Corporation, where he held a number of engineering and production management positions, including Vice President of Production at the Company's Fort Worth Division and Assistant General Manager of Engineering at the Electric Boat Division. Dr. Ashton introduced new technology to cut the number of manhours in building the F-16 aircraft by nearly 50 percent.

JAMES A. BAKER

Executive Vice President and Sector Executive, Technical Systems Sector, General Electric Company. This Sector includes electronic components, medical systems, aerospace, mobile communications, electric motors and industrial electronics businesses. Mr. Baker is a major force behind the company's broad-based thrust into advanced manufacturing systems. He was instrumental in GE's acquisition of Calma, Intersil and CAE International. He is a shaker and mover for new businesses like the robotics operation, as well as technology transfers. After joining GE in 1952, he held a series of engineering and sales assignments; was elected a company Vice President; became Group Executive of the Lighting Business Group; and later took over the Industrial Products and Components Sector.

ERICH BLOCH

Vice President, International Business Machines Corporation. Mr. Bloch participated in the development of IBM's first computers and then in their application to manufacturing systems, which is responsible for today's computer proliferation. He has been Director of IBM's Poughkeepsie Laboratory and Director of Large System Development. In 1970, he became Vice President, Operations, IBM Components Division, and was subsequently a Vice President of the Data Systems Division and General Manager of East Fishkill. In both positions he was responsible for the development and manufacture of semiconductor logic and memory components used in most of IBM's product line. He is presently concerned with promoting the technical vitality of IBM's professional engineering, programming, technology and scientific communities throughout the world.

H.E. BOVAY, JR.

Chairman and Chief Executive Officer, Bovay Engineers, Inc. This is a professional consulting firm performing worldwide master planning and engineering assignments leading toward factory-of-the-future concepts. Mr. Bovay is also President of the Mid-South Telephone Company, Lamar County Telephone Company, and Bovista Farms. He is a member and past-President of the National Society of Professional Engineers, and a member of the National Academy of Engineering.

LEO H. EVERITT, JR.

Vice President-Manufacturing, FMC Corporation. Mr. Everitt's areas of responsibility include Materials Management, Quality Assurance, Manufacturing Planning and Development, Employee Involvement/Increasing Value, Environmental Planning, Transportation, National Contract Purchasing and Real Estate, all of which aid line management in improving operating effectiveness. He has had extensive industrial and consulting experience, having progressed through increasingly responsible positions at such companies as General Electric Company and Cummins Engine Company, where he was Vice President-Organization Effectiveness.

VINCENT E. GIULIANO

Vice President and Chief Scientist, Mirror Systems, Inc.—a new Times-Mirror Company, committed to the development of innovative software for microcomputers and videodiscs. He has been concerned with the handling of information since 1952, and was the first person to introduce the use of digital computers to the General Motors Engineering Staff in 1953. Until recently he was Senior Information Sytems Specialist at Arthur D. Little, Inc., where he was particularly concerned with office automation, strategic planning required to introduce it, and the practical challenges associated with making it real. He has led strategic planning studies for two major corporations, specifically oriented toward creation of an overall framework for information and office automation. To aid the business strategy of an office equipment manufacturer, Dr. Giuliano undertook a study defining paths toward the development of the "office of the future."

JOEL D. GOLDHAR

Dean, School of Business Administration, Illinois Institute of Technology; Consultant, Joel D. Goldhar Management Consultants, Inc. During his recent service as Executive Director of the Manufacturing Studies Board, National Research Council (1980-1982) he came to be acknowledged as a key source of information about all active far longer/the-future projects. In addition he has been Executive Secretary, Committee on Computational Mechanics (1981-1982); Executive Secretary, Committee on Computer-Aided Manufacturing (1978-1981); and Program Director for User Requirements, Division of Science Information of the National Science Foundation. Dr. Goldhar's teaching experiences include Rensselaer Polytechnic Institute and the Harvard Business School.

M. WILLIAM GRANT

Vice President, Ingersoll-Rand Company. He is currently responsible for Corporate Manufacturing, Facilities, Purchasing, Transportation and Systems. In 1947, Mr. Grant began his career with Ingersoll-Rand in the Tool Design Department of the firm's Athens, Pennsylvania plant. He became Plant Superintendent of the Athens plant in 1959 and General Manager in 1963. He was named Manager of Manufacturing on the headquarters executive staff in 1965, and a Vice President of the Company in 1969. Mr. Grant is the chairman of the MAPI Manufacturing Council and the Director of the National Council of Northeastern University.

GEORGE A. HARTER

Vice President, Planning and Investment, TRW Inc. TRW has 90 divisions and a formidable mix of manufacturing operations. His department has corporate responsibility for strategic planning, acquisitions, mergers, capital expenditures, and for investment in major new products, plants and programs. Mr. Harter joined TRW in 1957, and held a number of key technical and managerial positions in the spacecraft and electronics fields. He was promoted to Vice President and Assistant General Manager of TRW Defense & Space Systems Group in 1977, and assumed his current responsibility in 1982. Mr. Harter is a member of the National Academy of Engineering (NAE), and chairman of NAE's Space Applications Board, which serves in an advisory capacity to the NASA Associate Administrator for Space Applications.

JAMES F. LARDNER

Vice President, Government Products and Component Sales, Deere & Company. During the decade of the 1970's, Mr. Lardner held the position of Director of Manufacturing Engineering. Deere emerged from that decade a leader in the application of integrated computer systems to manufacturing and won an award from the Society of Manufacturing Engineers for its computerized Tractor Works at Waterloo, Iowa. He joined the firm in 1946, and subsequently held a variety of positions before assuming his present post in 1982. He is responsible for original equipment and technology sales. Mr. Lardner is a member of the Computer Aided Manufacturing Advisory Group (CAMAG); the Computer and Automated Systems Association of the Society of Manufacturing Engineers; and the Manufacturing Management Council of that organization.

ROBERT J. MAYER

Vice President, Booz, Allen & Hamilton Inc. Mr. Mayer also serves as Managing Officer of the firm's Operations Management Services. He has concentrated in the area of manufacturing strategy with particular experience in the discrete products of the automotive and aerospace industries. He is a certified management consultant, former Vice President of the Institute of Management Consultants, and a member of its board of directors. He has served as Chairman of the Engineers Joint Council's Technology Assessment Panel; on the National Academy of Engineers' Committee on Computer-Aided Manufacturing to the Air Force; and is a member of the Computer Aided Manufacturing Advisory Group to the Air Force.

M. EUGENE MERCHANT

Director, Advanced Manufacturing Research, Metcut Research Associates Inc. Dr. Merchant joined Metcut in 1983, after retiring from Cincinnati Milacron Inc. He first joined the latter firm in 1936, and subsequently held a number of positions of responsibility including Assistant Director of Research (1951-1957); Director of Scientific Research (1957-1969); Director of Planning (1969-1981); and Principal Scientist, Manufacturing Research (1981-1983). In this last position, he toured the world to assess progress in advanced manufacturing systems. Dr. Merchant is a member of the National Academy of Engineering; an honorary member and past-president of the Society of Manufacturing Engineers; and a member of the American Society of Mechanical Engineers.

THOMAS J. MURRIN

President, Energy and Advanced Technology Group, Westinghouse Electric Corporation. Mr. Murrin is widely known for his tough, long-term insistence on across-the-board quality in manufacturing. He joined Westinghouse in 1951, and has subsequently held various positions of increasing responsibility both in the United States and overseas. He was President of Westinghouse Public Systems Company from 1975 to 1983. After a major reorganization of the firm, he is now responsible for worldwide operations in defense, nuclear energy systems, advanced electronics, and power generation. Mr. Murrin is a member and past-chairman of the Board of Governors of the Aerospace Industries Association, and a member of the Secretary of Defense's Defense Policy Advisory Committee on Trade.

STEPHEN R. ROSENTHAL

Professor of Operations Management, Boston University School of Management. Professor Rosenthal has been on the faculty of Boston University since 1975. For 20 years he has been involved in various aspects of the management of technology. He recently completed a major study of the adoption and implementation of factory automation technology in the United States. Professor Rosenthal also serves as a consultant to major manufacturing organizations and government agencies. In his prior professional positions he developed planning models for Exxon; formulated research support policy as a program officer for the National Science Foundation; and assessed policies and programs for several different government agencies. He has held visiting faculty appointments at Princeton, Brandeis, Columbia and Harvard Universities.

THOMAS L. SKELLY

Vice President, Operations, Wangtek Company, a start-up operation. Before assuming his present position in 1983, Mr. Skelly was Vice President of Manufacturing, Office Products Division, Xerox Corporation, where he was involved in simultaneous development of a totally new product line and creation of manufacturing facilities rapidly responsive to marketing strategies for that line. Earlier, he was Vice President of Manufacturing for Century Data Systems, a manufacturer of rotating disk memory systems. From 1977 to 1979, he was Vice President of Manufacturing of the Memory Products Division of California Computer. Mr. Skelly was previously associated with Mergenthaler Linotype Company, Computer Machinery Corporation, and RCA.

LEIGHTON F. SMITH

Partner, Director of Industry Education, Arthur Andersen & Co. Mr. Smith was in charge of Arthur Andersen's consulting practice in Japan from 1976 to 1982, a period during which that country's manufacturing systems underwent a major change. He has had a wide range of experience in the development of computerized systems in many industries. His work in Japan involved the design and installation of manufacturing planning and control systems for many Japanese manufacturing companies, including Yamaha Motor, Stanley Electric, Makita Electric Works, Tomy Toys, and Hitachi. He joined Arthur Andersen & Co. in 1948, and became partner in charge of the Management Consulting Division in 1969.

HAYWARD THOMAS

Senior Vice President, Broan Manufacturing—A Nortek Company. Mr. Thomas joined the firm in his present position in 1973. Previously, he served as Group Vice President of White Motor Corporation (1971), and before that as Vice President of Manufacturing. He is the vice chairman of the Manufacturing Council of the Society of Manufacturing Engineers. Mr. Thomas takes a temperate approach to high technology, firmly advocating Yankee ingenuity in the manufacturing process that has put his company in a high competitive posture.

HARRY B. THOMPSON

Principal, A.T. Kearney, Inc. Mr. Thompson has been with the firm for 12 years and has focused his attention on the management of manufacturing operations. He is well-known for his forthright views on manufacturing policy issues. Among his areas of emphasis are manufacturing strategy, the adoption of new technology, and facilities planning. Before joining Kearney, he was the Manager of manufacturing engineering for the Power Controls Division of Midland Ross Corporation.

JACK WICKHAM

President, The J.L. Wickham Co., Inc.—a manufacturing systems and consulting firm specializing in high-speed processing and assembly systems for volume production. The J.L. Wickham Company is a producer of unique system elements for flexible manufacturing. From 1968 to 1982, Mr. Wickham was affiliated with The Black & Decker Manufacturing Company in various positions of responsibility including Development Manager and Senior Technical Manager, Manufacturing Technology R&D. He is a senior member of the Society of Manufacturing Engineers.

[1]His colleagues, including the participants in this project, were saddened by Bill Abernathy's death in December, 1983. The Conference Board is grateful to his colleague, Alan Kantrow, Associate Editor of the *Harvard Business Review,* who checked the accuracy of this paper for us.

Why This Report

Improving manufacturing competitiveness is a vital objective of many U.S. businesses today. How can productivity and product quality be improved and production costs reduced to meet increasing competition? New technology to help companies achieve these goals is at hand. But beyond choosing appropriate equipment and systems, management, in setting them into place, faces a host of tough challenges—challenges such as retraining the work force, supervisors, technicians and middle management; rearranging work flow; improving performance of suppliers; establishing closer linkages among production and other functions; financing equipment purchases; and, perhaps the toughest of all, reexamining traditional assumptions about how the company ought to be managed.

In May of 1983, The Conference Board convened a conference on "Meeting the New Industrial Competition" at which a group of experts from industry, the consulting profession, and education discussed new concepts and new technology in manufacturing and their significance. We have prepared this synthesis of that event.

We are grateful to the individuals listed on pages vii-ix both for participating in the conference and for permitting us to include in this volume a distillation of their thoughts.

JAMES T. MILLS
President

Prologue

"It must be remembered that there is nothing more difficult to plan, more uncertain of success, nor more dangerous to manage than the creation of a new order of things. For the initiator has the enmity of all who would profit by the preservation of the old institutions, and merely lukewarm defenders in those who would gain by the new ones."

—Machiavelli, *The Prince* (1513)

Never before have companies faced such crucial challenges to participating successfully in world markets for manufactured goods. Not only have strong foreign competitors emerged, but markets are changing: Customers are more demanding; products are more sophisticated; and product life-cycles are shortening.

A means of meeting these challenges is at hand. Advanced manufacturing technology and systems that are closely coupled to an organization's vital functions—and to its suppliers and markets—give industry the power to:

- Respond more immediately to customer demand for model mixes;
- Reduce the cost of offering greater product variety;
- Penetrate profitably markets for relatively low-volume goods; and
- Deliver consistent quality of product.

No longer does the capability to be competitive and profitable depend on economies of scale alone. Successful strategies can be built on the economics of diversity or scope.

Informed commentators maintain that exploitation of the new technology and systems is essential if U.S. manufacturing industry is to regain its competitive strength. (In one memorable formulation, the alternatives are "to automate, emigrate to low labor-cost countries or evaporate.") Yet this will not be an easy task. Adopting the new technology and systems is likely to prove economically disappointing—and, for some firms, perhaps even disastrous—without careful examination of their myriad consequences—some counterintuitive; and without extensive changes in management policies and practices, not just on the factory floor but elsewhere in the organization.

The importance of these issues—the promise and pitfalls of "the factory of the future"—led The Conference Board to sponsor a session in the Spring of 1983 on "Meeting the New Industrial Competition." Because of the value of what 21 distinguished speakers and chairmen said on that occasion and the interest with which it was received, it was deemed worthwhile to give broader dissemination, through this publication, of their experiences and views. This brief essay encapsulates them.

What the New Technology Portends

Thanks to the almost breathtaking progress in microelectronics, it is practical to distribute computing power throughout the factory. Thus, manufacturing is becoming an increasingly science-based activity. Because of the economic and marketing pluses of the new technology, decisions about it should transcend the production function. They should be corporatewide and strategic in nature—as they have been in those Japanese companies widely regarded as role models.

Yet that alone does not account for Japanese preeminence in manufacturing. Underlying it are managerial policies and practices that are not only essential for the successful utilization of new technology, but are also fruitful in *any* manufacturing environment. Among them: demanding quality standards, relatively few job categories, considerable decision making by individual workers on the factory floor, very low inventories of raw material and supplies.

Understanding and Action Needed

If management chooses to automate instead of emigrating or evaporating, what will this involve in terms of understanding and action? Perhaps the first thing to be done is to recognize and overcome the barriers that may be encountered. Prominent among them are: the parochial, functional outlook of many managers; preoccupation with cost reduction as the justification for investment; inadequately trained workers and supervisors; and fear of lost jobs, union problems, cost overruns.

Requirements for achieving superior manufacturing performance include: visible, top-down commitment by senior management; the development of a plan to ensure well-coordinated introduction of technology and attendant organizational change; assurance of adequate resources to do the job; and an integrated view of manufacturing, from concept design through field service of the finished product. Yet, despite the "big picture" character of these requirements, a gradual approach—"walking before running"—to the introduction of the technology itself is likely to be the answer for most companies. For them the issue, after all, is not building factories from scratch but improving the performance of existing plants. Suggested steps include getting a champion; forming a task force; beginning with an "island of automation."

The new technology will surely be expensive, even if management avoids the common error of buying more capability than it needs. But evaluation of the investment should be broader than the traditional marginal benefit analysis (e.g., "What payroll savings will installation of this machine make possible?") Savings attributable to reduced inventories and improved finished-product quality should be taken into account. So, too, should synergistic benefits like the opportunity to make new as well as existing products on new machinery. Finally, the risk associated with *not* making the investment must be recognized: Will the company suffer loss of market share if its competitors have the benefits of new technology and it does not?

In putting new technology in place, several mistakes must be guarded against. Among them are underutilization of machinery, poor methods engineering, and failure to draw suppliers into the effort.

Human Resources Issues

Central to the successful adoption of the new technology and systems are human-resources issues. Several stand out:

• The work force will have to be used effectively and efficiently, which means that jobs will have to be redefined and the shortage of critical skills will have to be remedied by reeducation and training. For major, technology-dependent companies, part of the latter effort will entail support of innovation in engineering and other technical schools.

• Management must keep in mind, both in its own decision making and in guiding employees, that productivity and quality are not in conflict, that better quality enhances productivity and vice versa.

• Much has to be done in the way of motivating workers to accept and capitalize on the new technology: participative management, quality circles, productivity programs, and the abandonment of authoritative relationships between supervisors and those supervised.

• Middle management, no longer required to spend considerable time processing information for top management, must become technically more competent and more capable of directing large segments of an organization.

• Top management will probably have to adopt a new style. In most companies, management style has been conducive to preserving stability, but not to effecting change. Utilizing the new technology will be frustrating if top management is inflexible, risk-adversive, unforgiving.

In summary, everyone will have a new role: workers on the factory floor, supervisors, support staff, middle management, and top executives. The challenge will be precisely that defined by Machiavelli.

James K. Brown
Executive Director,
Management Functions
Program Group

Part I
An Overview

Characteristics of New Concept Factories
Joel D. Goldhar

The issues of productivity, manufacturing, industrialization, the pursuit of excellence, and so on, have at last reached the public agenda for discussion in the trade press, in the business press, in the daily newspapers, and on television. Operations and manufacturing have again become an important driving force for new corporate strategy, for changes in the way in which our companies are run and, possibly, for changes in the backgrounds of the people who run our companies.

Students keep asking me what career path to take. If I knew the answer, I would really not be a dean. But it does seem that we may be ready to turn from lawyers and accountants to operations managers and manufacturing executives to run our companies.

Four Basic Ideas

To understand the implications of modern manufacturing, four basic ideas require consideration. The first is that the new manufacturing technology is fundamentally different in design, in operation, and in capability from the equipment, process and technology that we are accustomed to in traditional factories. The new technology is smarter, faster, close-coupled, integrated, optimized and flexible. We are going to have to become accustomed to a whole new lexicon of buzz words, very different from those that we used in traditional manufacturing and engineering.

The new factory not only does traditional tasks differently, it can perform tasks not possible in the traditional factory. This means that many of the opportunities that we face, the management styles we need to use, the strategic options that are available to us, and the production decisions that we have to make are going to be contrary to the experience of past successes.

Second, the marketplace is changing in a very basic way and will demand the kinds of capability that the new technology can deliver (see pages 2-3). Short life-cycle products, fragmented markets, and international competition combine to create a fundamental structural shift in both industrial and consumer markets.

Third, manufacturing is rapidly becoming a science-based activity, with high potential for revolutionary change—well beyond what is considered even today as the state of the art. We are about to go beyond the situation when to say, "I'm a manufacturing engineer," was a euphemism for not having a college degree and for coming up from the plant floor. The level of scientific and technical capabilities required to truly understand how to design, manage and optimize the kinds of factories we are discussing are well beyond even what most college-trained manufacturing engineers possess. Trends in materials science, control theory, and artificial intelligence, combined with the application of computers and communications technology and information science techniques will lead us to the new concept of manufacturing at its most powerful level.

Computer-integrated manufacturing (CIM) embraces fully integrated, close-coupled, high-variety but continuous-flow systems in which lead times for new product introductions or improvements will be drastically reduced. Work-in-progress inventories will practically disappear; costly final-goods inventories, used to buffer the factory from the uncertainties of the marketplace, will not be as necessary; and both direct and indirect labor will be substantially reduced.

A word of warning is appropriate, however. The new technology is a computer-aided way to do the things we always recognized as necessary to run an effective factory. But if management is not running an effective factory now, no amount of computer automation is going to help. If the industrial engineering is sloppy, if the standards are loose, if the layout is poor, if the production planning and control systems are not up to the standards of today's best practices, if the product designs are old—then simply putting everything on the computer is not going to help very much. The advent of the new technology allows us to do these things better, and provides a stimulus for thinking through proper methods and procedures in management techniques.

The CIM factory is a paperless factory. It is a match between computer-controlled hardware that is adaptable, flexible and multifunctional, and paperless knowledge work capabilities that allow us to manage large amounts of information in real time, to handle variety, quick change, and flexibility and to take advantage of the true power of the new factory hardware. One without the other is not sufficient. Quick-change hardware without an information system that allows one to keep track of the variety he or she is dealing with will cause trouble, and a fancy information system that is faster than hardware can change is not going to deliver its full value.

Making effective use of this technology will require new marketing styles and corporate strategies emphasizing rapid design changes, customization of products, and new techniques for the design and management of factories that take into account the unique features of computer-integrated manufacturing.

We also need to rethink most of our traditional concepts of factory organization, plant layout, facilities location, choice of process technology and equipment, production planning and control techniques, degree of standardization of product designs, length of run, size of batch, line versus staff responsibilities, the factory's focus or lack of it, the means for introducing new technology into existing systems, how to measure productivity and performance, and the training and skills needed by managers and professionals. Everything is up for reappraisal.

That is not to say that everything is going to change. It is to say that everything has to be looked at with a fresh eye to find out whether or not it has to change.

Fourth, the influences of this new manufacturing technology extend throughout the firm. They go far beyond the factory and have a major impact on the competitive strategies available to the firm. The market and product trends in worldwide competition require these new strategies if U.S. industry is to remain a leader or, perhaps more accurately, to regain its leadership, in manufacturing.

Manufacturing technology decisions are now, therefore, corporatewide and strategic in nature. That is a very big change from the past—a change that is driven by the realities of today's market and today's technology; and one I think is long overdue. This change will, however, call for some major adjustments in top-management leadership style, in organization design, in the flows of information and decision making in the company, and, probably, in a realignment of the "division of turf" within traditionally organized companies.

Key Competitive and Technological Trends

What are the driving factors behind the current U.S. emphasis on manufacturing as a competitive weapon? They include declining productivity and market share; aging factories and facilities; outmoded engineering and business school faculties and their impact on the new generation of engineers and managers; and the short-term financial emphasis that has been bemoaned, documented and lip-serviced almost to death. There is also a lack of sufficient investment and innovation in manufacturing-process technology, despite what we see at the leading-edge companies. In my own city, Chicago, and elsewhere, one can see many examples of factories of the past without much of a future.

Internationalization

Three other key trends complete the context for a discussion of the new importance of manufacturing. The first is the increasing internationalization of everything—competition, markets, production, technology and innovation. It needs to be emphasized again that the United States no longer has a lock on innovation. And our competitors are not confined to Japan, Taiwan and Korea. The kind of technology I am talking about is movable to Malaysia, Sri Lanka, India, Kenya—anywhere in the world. I think we need to be concerned about the next set of emerging competitors. We have to stop worrying about whether we can copy what Japan has done well in the last ten years, because that is probably not good for the next ten years, or is as bad for the next ten years as our own practices have been. We need to start looking at the demands in the marketplace of the future.

Changing Markets

The second trend is that the market is changing in a very fundamental way. We are moving toward a marketplace that is probably best described by Alvin Toffler in *The Third Wave*, when he talks about "demassification."[1] It is important to get a sense of the profile of the markets in which the company does business: the profile now, and the profile in the next five, ten, fifteen or twenty years. In general, all markets appear to be moving in the direction of shorter, more truncated product life cycles. Computer chips now seem to have a year-and-a-half to a three-year life cycle. Similarly, a product line with an

[1]Alvin Toffler, *The Third Wave*. New York: William Morrow & Co., 1980.

eighteen-year life cycle is moving toward twelve; one with a twelve-year life cycle is moving toward six. If it had a six-year life cycle, it is moving to three. If it had a three-year life cycle, people will start talking about months. Those who worry about matching up the product and process life cycle now need to change their ideas, because the product life cycle is not going to be long enough or leisurely enough to allow a change in the design of the factory. The factory that a product starts in is the factory in which it is going to die. And that factory will have to be usable for a sequence of product designs.

More complex and more rapidly changing product technology and increasingly complex levels of technology in our products are putting new demands on manufacturing. If anybody had told executives in the appliance business 15 years ago that a decade or two later all of their products would have electronic computers inside them, and that most products would talk back to their users, these executives would have said the prophet was crazy.

My own design for the next "hot new product" is the computer-controlled running shoe with a pressure transducer, a customized chip for my weight and running habits, and a little red light in the toe, so that when I am running too far or too fast (rarely does that happen, of course) it will start to beep and tell me I am putting too much stress on my fibula. And if the shoe has not been used in two or three days, it will start to beep and a nice little voice will say, "Happy birthday to you, get your act together and run." Imagine what this means to the production manager at a traditional shoe company in the United States—or in a developing country. It is not all bad news.

Consumers in the new marketplace are much more sophisticated and are demanding greater variety and customization in product designs. They are far more insistent on quality, reliability and innovation from their suppliers, and far less loyal in return than they were in the past. The basic buyer-seller relationship, in both industrial and consumer markets, is up for renegotiation. It is not clear how matters will turn out, but I do think the ability of the new technology to deliver customization and variety is going to make a difference for those companies that invest in it.

New Science and Technology

Third, the science and technology of manufacturing are becoming much more complex and far more powerful. We are developing a better understanding of the scientific underpinnings of production. Essentially that comes from better knowledge of the behavior of solid-state materials under various process conditions. As an analogy, we might ask why chemical companies have been willing to invest hundreds of millions of dollars in relatively unproven new process technology plants. It is, in my view, because we know enough about the behavior of matter in the fluid state to be able to design and optimize a new process on paper and in the computer, and to build a test-scale pilot plant before companies make large-scale investments. We do not have many pilot plants for mechanical-based technologies; nor do we have a sense of confidence in our scale-up factors. But we are getting there. We are beginning to learn more about how to simulate factory operations. We are beginning to get better tools. We certainly know more now about the behavior of materials that we are using in the design of factory and manufacturing systems. Control theory, artificial intelligence, measurement and sensing capabilities are all advancing at a very rapid rate.

This increasing scientific base really is leading toward a factory with *reduced process uncertainty*. Information always reduces uncertainty; and that is what is happening in the CIM factory. We are moving toward what has been called data-intensive manufacturing. Data reduce uncertainty, and that, in turn, makes the factory more predictable and more controllable, much more like a chemical plant, but, as I will explain later, with some very important differences in its fundamental economics.

The application of electronic computers and communications technology and information science to all aspects of manufacturing, from control of the physical conversion and movement of materials to the design, planning and managerial knowledge work of the factory, is, of course, becoming more common. Add to this the concepts of group technology and the availability of three-dimensional geometric models that link computer-aided design and engineering to computer-aided manufacturing and computer-assisted management. The result is a totally new concept in manufacturing: Making factories predictable, controllable and subject to mathematical modeling and optimization—that is to say, a science-based manufacturing system.

This new manufacturing will be at its most powerful when the computer and communications technologies are used with increased scientific understanding of materials and processes to link production processes and management tasks in that fully integrated, close-coupled, continuous-flow, still utopian (but not for much longer) factory of the future. Computer-integrated manufacturing is central to the factory of the future—a combination of hardware and software and a data base describing the physical phenomena that allow someone to write a computer program that models the factory, and communications to provide on-line variable programs, flexible automation, on-line, moment-by-moment schedule and performance optimization, and dynamic reallocation of resources. It is, in a sense, the "perfect information" factory. We are not quite there yet, but at least now we can set the standard for the future.

Conceptual Base

These capabilities suggest that the "factory of the future" really combines three ideas. It is a continuous flow of product like a chemical plant, but it is based on "economy of scope," allowing the production of a variety of similar products in random order. And it has economy of scale in technology and distribution derived from the overall volume of operations.

Even more importantly, one needs to think about the factory of the future as a computer system in which the peripherals, instead of being printers, plotters, terminals and disc packs, are robots, machine tools, and other process equipment. It is little noisier and a little messier, but it is basically a computer system. The ongoing discussions of the pros and cons of centralized production facilities, of product versus process factory focus, and so on, are exactly analogous to the arguments we have had over the last 20 years on distributed versus centralized computing and data processing. This makes sense because the technology is indeed the same. The fundamental problems are not technological ones. They are managerial and organizational. People who grew up with mechanical engineering as their base technology now have to yield to computer scientists and electrical engineers.

We are switching from an era in which we produced large volumes of standard products on specialized machinery to systems for the production of a wide variety of similar products in small batches—even one at a time—on technology that is standard but multimission, flexible and tailored to the particular design through software. When information is in machine-readable form, rather than built into conveyors or pipes or cams and gears, we have the flexible capabilities for the factories we are talking about. These combinations of computer systems and chemical-plant flows with their attributes of scope, flexibility and close coupling will allow U.S. industry to respond to the market pressures of the future.

Economy of Scope and Factory Operations

The key to understanding the opportunities presented by flexible manufacturing is a set of production economics concepts called *economy of scope*. It is an idea that comes from the literature on the economics of information. For example, one does not need a million copies of a single journal to support a printing press or, in fact, to support an economic analysis department. Rather, one needs a thousand copies of 100 to 1,000 different journals that all want to report some part of the same information tailored to a specific audience. Economy of scope allows for low-cost variety of output, and that is the basic physical and philosophical difference between new and old factories. What this means is that the cost of producing a bundle of different product configurations on a particular piece of multimission equipment is the same as, or, more like-

ly, less than, the cost of producing the same number of pieces of identical design on specialized equipment designed for that particular product configuration.

The best example is a simple numerical control machine tool or CNC machining center. Such a tool can equally well make 12 of one product design in a row, or one each of 12 different designs in random order, provided those 12 different designs have been incorporated into its software. Essentially, this moves the fixed cost per design away from the plant floor and back to the engineering stage—and leads us to some generalizations on the design and characteristics of the factory of the future.

A new concept factory will be characterized by information in machine-readable form, multimission smart tools, and paperless management systems. It will be an essentially 100-percent fixed-cost system. It will have a flat learning curve and high levels of investment in software and maintenance. These characteristics are exactly opposite to those we have strived to build into our plants in the past.

A factory based on economy of scope rather than of scale will require a switch in management emphasis from minimum cost to maximum effectiveness and profitability. It will entail a very real change in the way we talk about productivity and in the role of the factory manager.

In practice, these factories could operate with an economic order quantity of one. Variety will have no cost penalty, at least on the production floor, but cost per unit will be very sensitive to volume because total costs are essentially fixed. The factory will be capable of high levels of accuracy and repeatability. However, these cost-of-variety advantages will do little good for a company that is selling long runs of standard products with (assumed) long life cycle.

The factory is going to be essentially unmanned, capable of rapid changes in design and in production rates—probably more capable than are its managers. Quality will be built in from the beginning. It will be based on joint cost rather than marginal cost economics. If the factory is thought of as a computer system, capacity additions will in be relatively small increments. Once the basic computer capability has been built, the software to add another milling machine or another robot cart or another loop on the line can be put in place quickly enough to eliminate any long-range capacity planning concerns. We are going toward what is essentially virtually unlimited capacity, analogous to "virtual memory."

Traditional line managers' responsibilities for productivity will move to what we now consider staff; or, alternatively, we had better redefine who is staff and who is line and who is responsible for productivity. Management's attention will be focused on extensive and very expensive preproduction activities, rather than on the plant floor.

This will lead to some organizational and strategic implications for the firm as a whole and runs counter to some of our current thinking about the need to focus on the factory floor. This new level of attention to the factory must be in terms of its strategic importance and its technology rather than having a human relations emphasis. The "people management" problems will involve managing professionals and managing organizational change.

Organizationally, there will be fewer but higher-skilled and better-paid employees. New criteria for pay and other rewards will have to be established. More attention will have to be paid to training. A new accounting system will be needed to manage the plant. If we retain an accounting system that is based on overhead against direct labor, that sole person in the control room will have 977,000 percent overhead loaded against him or her. This may be technically correct, but it is not very useful as a tool for manufacturing management.

Impacts on Capital Budgeting

Firms will require a new style of capital budgeting that encourages process innovation. For example, most capital budgeting systems now ask: With that machine, what would it have cost us to run the plant last year? The difference is taken between that figure and the actual cost; that amount is divided by the cost of the investment; a net present value calculation is made; then a go or no-go decision is made. But this approach overlooks the fact that last year's product mix was based on what last year's factory could do well, which was long runs and standard products. If one assumes long runs of standard products on equipment that represents a heavy investment in flexibility, variety and quick-change capability, it is not surprising that the return on investment is probably lower. Markets, products, performance and process technology need to be matched in the capital-budgeting exercise.

The questions are: What will the product mix be five or ten years from now? What will it cost to make that product mix on traditional equipment? Inevitably, companies are moving toward proliferated product lines and short product-life cycles. When the market goes in that direction, then the next question is: What will it cost to meet the market demands if the company does not make the investment in new manufacturing technology—the hardware, the software, and the management capability that will be required?

New Management Styles

New concepts of traditional engineering and production management will be needed as well. The manufacturing manager of the future will have to shift attention from the traditional narrow focus on productivity and unit material and labor costs to: (1) integration within the factory and integration among R&D, engineering, the factory, marketing and distribution; (2) innovation, both process innovation and product innovation; and (3) strategy for the manufacturing function and the contribution of manufacturing to the strategic thrust of the firm as a whole. Let us examine briefly how the manager's working environment and decision-making structure will change.

The traditional factory was based on concepts of batch, scale and the experience curve. Task specialization was desirable; work was a social activity; one could calculate the variable costs; and it was desirable to standardize. In the "CAD-CAM-CIM factory of the future," all this will be different. The watchwords will be flow process, scope, truncated product-life cycles, multimission equipment, unmanned systems, joint costs, and variety of output.

For the old factory sound operating principles and management techniques consonant with the old assumptions were developed: Centralization, large plants, balanced lines, smooth flow, standard product design, low rate of change, and inventory as a decoupler from the market were all desirable characteristics of the "good" factory.

The new factory will be marked by an entirely different set of desirable operating characteristics: decentralization, disaggregation, flexibility, rapid conversion of product lines produced, surge and "turn-aroundability," responsiveness to innovation, production tied to demand, multiple functions, and close-coupled systems. These represent sharp changes both for practitioners of manufacturing engineering and teachers of manufacturing management. The new factory will change the definition of productivity to one based on these variables.

Other demands to be put on the new factory and included in the definition of productivity are: minimal downtime for maintenance; maximum product-family range; the ability to adapt variability in materials and process conditions; the ability to handle increasingly complex product designs and technology; and the ability to integrate new process technology into the existing systems with minimum disruption and minimum cost. The factory of the future is as likely to be a high-cost factory (capable of dominating the fashion market segment through rapid product design change) as a low-cost price leader. A narrow preoccupation with cost and traditionally measured productivity will not get us where we need to go. However, new strategic options are possible.

Strategies for Maximizing Value

All of these new operating characteristics and changing criteria for manufacturing success lead to a set of strategies for maximizing the value of the factory of the future that is mainly counterintuitive to the strategies that have worked for us in the past.

The first of these new strategies is to invest in flexible manufacturing technology. That is the big gamble: to fundamentally change the manufacturing capabilities of the firm and to make manufacturing the basis for competitive advantage.

Second, a company has to take control of the market. The CIM factory will require competitive strategies that build on the strength inherent in the technology. They will include *deliberate* efforts to proliferate product designs, to truncate and shorten the product-life cycle, deliberate use of distributed and fragmented production locations closer to customers, and emphasis on quality and reliability as measures of value. The notion that everything falls apart at the same time will no longer be a model for engineering analysis.

Many of our marketing strategies are based on inherent assumptions about what existing factories will do well: long runs of standard products over a long period of time in which change is barred at the door. I am convinced that one reason factories are located in Peoria, in Erie, and in Dubuque is so that change can not find its way to them. We keep R&D in Boston, Silicon Valley, Westchester County, and Phoenix—all at great distances from the factories. This has been understandable. The manufacturing manager was instructed to deliver a specified product on time, at acceptable quality, on spec, and, most importantly, at the lowest possible cost. Product design, people, process technology, and the accounting system were not to be changed; if any of them were, it would cost the company money. And the manufacturing manager was rewarded on the basis of minimum cost per unit.

Consider, for example, the traditional market segmentation strategy: If we focus on this particular market segment and build a well-engineered traditional factory, there is enough scale in that market segment for us to make progress down on the learning curve and compete in a traditional way. That little market can be won away from a larger firm that is dealing in a more broadly defined market segment. What has to be done in the future is to fragment the market so much that no segment is large enough to allow that kind of "cherry picking." Finally, compete broadly across the market segments, taking advantage of broad-scope manufacturing capabilities, large-scale product design and engineering and massive distribution capabilities. Do everything possible to build competitive advantage based on the strengths of this technology that also minimize the strengths of either less aggressive firms or of offshore competitors.

One vital question about traditional strategic approaches concerns the number-two firm in the industry. Number Two was traditionally an attractive position. The pioneer—Number One—had an arrow in its back, its face in the mud, and a low P/E ratio. Number Two did not have to test the market; perhaps it could make the product cheaper or better. In the future it may be that because that product's life cycle is going to move so fast and the market is going to be so thin, there will not be a Number Two. The company that chooses to invest in flexibility and aggressively change the nature of the market is going to dominate it. If there is, for structural reasons, still a Number Two, there is not likely to be a Number Three.

Third, we need to build competitive advantage into the R&D, engineering and distribution systems. For the next ten or twenty years, competitive advantage will come from investing in the new manufacturing technology. But when everybody has it and there are managers and engineers who know what to do with it, then manufacturing will be a leveler. What, then, will be the source of competitive advantage? It will be in R&D, engineering, product design, marketing and distribution. The point is not to wait for ten years, but to begin now to develop these strengths, taking care to integrate these advantages into an overall strategic competitive posture..

Making It Happen

All this requires a top-down strategic approach. This kind of innovation is not going to bubble up from the plant floor. There has to be *commitment* starting with the board of directors and implemented across the organization. That means that a firm must have a well-thought-out strategy before it can effectively justify and utilize a factory of the future. It has taken me some time to realize what many people in industry have been saying: We have a plan; we have a book full of numbers; but we have never had a corporate strategy, a basic strategic thinking process that tells us how we are going to compete. So one has to start with a strategy. And it is the same strategy model that we have been teaching in business schools for years. It is: What business are we in or what business do we want to be in? *And what must we be able to do well to be successful in that business?* And then how can we acquire the necessary skills?

I am arguing that what *some* businesses need to be good at are those skills that can be acquired through the use of advanced manufacturing technology. Then the questions are: How do we exploit these skills? How do we protect our unique capability? How do we dominate that market long enough to get a return on investment, which by now is very, very large. (If those questions cannot be answered, then reiteration is necessary: Are we exploiting those skills properly? Have we acquired the right skills? Have we identified the proper skills? Or should we be in a different business?) Pondering these questions should reveal a corporate strategy that will allow the company to compete in the markets of the future, markets that will be driven by the capabilities inherent in the new manufacturing technology.

Part II
The Competitive Environment

Myths and Realities about Japanese Industry
Leighton F. Smith

My responsibility in Japan, where I worked from 1976 until 1982, was to drum up business for our consulting services. In the course of my work, I learned that most of my initial ideas for explaining the Japanese productivity and competitiveness—the ideas also held by many U.S. executives—are not true, or are not important. For example, lifetime employment in Japan is a myth. The hiring and firing goes on in the companies with fewer than 50 employees—that is where half the work force is found. In bad times, there are about 1,000 bankruptcies a week in Japan. These little companies go out of business as big companies pull in work to meet the lifetime employment guarantees to their own people.

One by one, other myths about wages and cheap labor and the work ethic were stripped away. What remained were corporate strategy and tactics made possible by effective integration of advanced manufacturing systems. The computer functioned as an agent of change, providing information for motivation and action.

The Yamaha Example

Yamaha Motors has a sales volume of $2 billion a year. It produces 1,700 different models of motorcycles worldwide. It makes 2,000 change orders a month, in parts to keep up with EPA regulations and similar regulations in other national markets, and it utilizes 200,000 parts in production.

Yamaha told me it wanted an MRP system. I proposed forming a team of Yamaha and Arthur Andersen people to study the company's present procedures so as to determine what ought to be put on the computer. The vice president of manufacturing demurred. "We are not going to take that approach," he said. "First, we are going to decide how we want to run our factory. Then we are going to decide how to deal with our suppliers, and fit them into that factory. Third, we shall determine how to

motivate our engineers to be more responsive to the market, to these engineering change orders and to new products. Once we have done all that, then we shall figure out what system we need to enforce those factory disciplines."

His reasoning: "Honda has 40 percent of the world market for motorcycles and we have 25 percent. We want to beat Honda and become number one. And to do that we must reduce the cost of goods manufactured by 25 percent. That is our goal. Realizing it will require us to combine MRP with Kanban (just-in-time production), the best of the East and the West, to motivate our middle management, foremen and workers so that they will accept the robots and other automation."

It took one month to plot the factory of the future at Yamaha and to figure out how production should be rearranged. There was no bottom-up contribution to this exercise; it was done right at the top.

The next step entailed turning over these ideas to middle-level management, which was told to determine how to carry them out. It took two years to resolve the details of what the new factory ought to look like and what the appropriate systems would be.

Before the factory could receive the new system it had to be "clean"—no inventory, no stockrooms. New projects were set up to accomplish this. The projects were turned over to well-trained foremen. There was a foreman's fund of about $6 to $12 million to be spent for robots, automation, set-up reduction, flow lines, standard containers, or relayout, at the discretion of the foremen—a modest sum, but it permitted each foreman to get involved.

For two years, then, the foremen ran their projects. Altogether, four years had gone by since plans for the new system had been made. When the Japanese convert to a new system the factory is ready, it is all cleaned up and everyone is behind it. The final conversion was completed in six months. Cost of sales was cut 3 percent, direct labor was cut by 10 percent, and $5 million was saved. A 15 percent reduction in indirect labor meant $3 million in savings. Inventory was cut 40 percent, saving $2 million in inventory carrying costs. The purchasing department contributed $30 million in savings, working closely with suppliers on long-term contracts and keying in just-in-time production.

Hitachi: A Formula for Market Success

How does a Japanese company decide to get into a new business? Hitachi is a $20 billion company with $2.4 billion in U.S. sales. In 1982, Hitachi put as much as $24 million into a plant for making 64-K random access memory chips. Two years earlier, management had decided that it wanted to get into this business. Now it has become a dominant factor, holding 40 percent of the world market. What was its formula for world dominance? Chips were selling for $24 at the time and Hitachi set a target price of $3 a chip. That was top management's goal: $3 a chip.

The quality standard set was zero failure in field performance. Then management subtracted from the selling price of $3 projected marketing costs and projected profit, leaving a manufacturing cost of $1. How could they make a chip for a dollar? It was concluded that the only way to do this was to improve first-time yield. Thomas J. Murrin has said that every dollar invested in cutting failures produces a return of four dollars (see page 43). There it was, in black and white, in Hitachi's strategy.

What did management do? It did not set the marketing people to do the task, or give it to the engineers, or turn it over to manufacturing. Instead, management brought all three groups together and said: "Figure it out, and don't come back until you have it." At the time (1981), the market for 64-K chips was $100 million. Hitachi management spent almost $30 million to go after a $100 million market because it was looking at the projected $1.5 billion market for 64-K chips by 1985. Someone has said that the Japanese do not do better long-range *planning,* but they are always *thinking* long range.

Comparison of Goals

A research study in which Stephen Rosenthal was prominently involved examined the future of manufacturing plans of companies in the United States, Japan and Europe.[1] The U.S. companies predominantly had soft goals. Number one was production inventory control systems (cited by 65 percent of the respondents). Supervisory training was number two. Integrated manufacturing management information systems was

number three (mentioned by 58 percent of the respondents). Some 50 percent of the respondents were planning to have quality circles in their companies. Direct-labor motivation did not make the list. These results suggest that U.S. firms are bent on making existing systems work better.

In Japan, the companies' goals involved hard stuff. Production inventory enforcing systems were first. This was followed by automating factory jobs (cited by 60 percent of the respondents); office automation, cited by 58 percent; new processes and new products, cited by 50 percent. Other goals included flexible manufacturing systems, which did not even get on the U.S. list of the top ten; reducing the size of the work force; introducing robots; giving workers broader tasks; and reconditioning the physical plant. European results fell between those in the United States and Japan.

We will never regain dominance in the world marketplace pursuing soft goals, while Japan is pursuing hard goals.

What We Should Learn from Japan
William J. Abernathy

In his book, *Germany Prepares for War,* Professor Banse offered this observation about industrial competence: "The psychological error lay in our conception of the American as a self-booster, a shoddy manufacturer of shoddy goods and an unscrupulous overreacher in business whose word cannot be trusted."[1]

Such Americans there certainly were. But there is another type of American who is conspicuously efficient in all industrial and technical undertakings: The American who builds the tallest buildings, produces the most motor cars, attains record economic output; who built the Panama Canal; and whose spirit and enterprise knows no bounds.

In fairness, we must admit that in the 1950's and 1960's a good part of U.S. industry was trying to prove true Banse's image of shoddy producer, shoddy merchandise. I fear we gave up our interest in production, turned our attention to finance and other issues, to the detriment of quality, productivity and product effectiveness.

A change is now occurring; there are signs of a renaissance. More and more companies are getting a firm hand on their production problems. Two main issues must be met if the renaissance is to flourish. The first is the management of technology; the second, the management of the work force. Both really come down to the management of people. I shall refer to the consumer electronics industry and the automobile industry as symbols of what has been happening in the United States.

[1]"The 1983 Global MFG Futures Study." Boston University, Waseda University (Japan), INSEAD/CEDEP (France).

[1]Ewald Banse, *Germany Prepares for War.* New York: Harcourt Brace Jovanovich, 1941.

Consumer Electronics

In 1955, the United States produced two-thirds of the world's capital goods and consumer electronics. We had recently developed the transistor. In 1957, Ampex introduced the video recorder, a brilliant innovation. We held most of the world's electronic capability and technical know-how. All indications were that the consumer electronics industry, then selling about $1.5 billion worth of TV sets a year, was poised for takeoff.

However, if one looks at the present-day consumer electronics products in U.S. households, most of them carry the labels of Panasonic, Hitachi or other Japanese firms. And if one looks closely at those with U.S. names, like Zenith, GE, or RCA, the consumer will discover that they were made in places like Taiwan and Hong Kong.

How could this have happened? A fashionable explanation has been that it is government's fault: It is overregulating; it is clearly spending too much money; it does not allow enough savings. Whatever the merit of these views, the consumer electronics industry has hardly been affected by government regulation. What no one has been saying is that perhaps it is a management problem.

In the mid-1950's, just two companies that I know of made little pocket radios, like the Dick Tracy wristwatch radio, and two companies made small transistorized pocket radios. The belief was that radios of this kind constituted a mature market. It was color television, computers, and other then-exotic devices that excited U.S. manufacturers.

Sony, not conversant with these "realities," began to produce portable transistorized radios that sold for about $200 apiece. The company made a lot of money. But, more than that, it began to suggest to the U.S. consumer that the Japanese could make something besides those little sparkly things put under Christmas trees. Sony also created new channels of distribution in the United States.

Much the same can be said of black-and white TV sets. Although the transistor was a U.S. invention, the Japanese were the first to transistorize TV. In the 1950's, the four-inch screen was common. But there was soon a push for bigger screens: Bigger and brighter were the watchwords. Definitive marketing research showed that there was absolutely no U.S. market for small TV sets. That was the mature end of the business. Sony, being absolutely stupid again, did not understand this. It built a small, transistorized TV set. Its ads showed a large, rotund gentleman lying back in bed with a big smile on his face and a small TV set on his tummy. That was how Sony successfully broke into the U.S. TV market—followed by other Japanese firms.

As color TV was developed, U.S. industry saw black-and-white TV as uninteresting and relegated it to offshore production, which greatly aided the industrial development of Asia. The Japanese, however, did not see black-and-white TV that way. Having produced highly reliable sets, they decided to make an end run around the franchised dealership network—the entry barrier to the U.S. market. Who would spend $200 or $300 for a TV set if there was no authorized local repairman to fix it? The Japanese sold their sets through mass channels of distribution, a solution which enabled them to capture a major stake in the U.S. television market. So the Japanese penetrated the electronics industry, and continued to infuse vitality into products that seemed mature. They won a lot of business while U.S. companies were asleep at the switch.

The most dramatic story, though, is the video recorder. According to legend, when this device was being introduced to television stations throughout the world, in the late 1950's, the chairman of Sony went with his chief engineer to the Japanese Broadcasting Network to see this very bulky marvel of technology, not suitable for use in the home. Recall that the Ampex video recorder was a console of equipment that cost $50,000 in 1957. It was a tape-gobbler, consuming 747 square feet of two-inch tape an hour. The chairman allegedly turned to the chief engineer and said: "That is a very interesting product. Your goal is to reduce the manufacturing cost 100-fold. It will make an interesting consumer product." Not from $50,000 to $5,000, but from $50,000 to $500. It took Sony 20 years, but the goal was achieved. In 1975, it introduced the Betamax. It consumed 20 square feet of half-inch tape an hour, and sold for $800; more recent models have been priced at $500.

How many of U.S. organizations could or would undertake a commitment of 20 years to achieve the kind of goal that Sony achieved in producing what I consider to be a brilliant consumer product, the home video recorder? And this commitment was made when Sony was a fairly small company. To be sure, it stumbled and fell along the way; but it got up and ran again.

Think about the whole U.S. consumer electronics industry, probably comprising 1,000 firms or more: How in the world could it have lost that important market segment to the Japanese—or to anyone else, for that matter? Somehow companies in this industry have not found a way to incorporate technology into their corporate strategy. They have not found a way to look on technology as a means of renewal. Why?

One reason is, I think, the high incidence of *Fortune 500* chief executive officers with financial backgrounds, many of whom have come to their posts from outside, without having worked their way up through the organization. Also, corporate executives have become increasingly disinterested in what goes on in product technology in manufacturing as they single-mindedly concentrate on profits. (See also page 20.) Consider what one hears when the brightest and the best young students speculate about their future careers. Most of them want "to go into finance," or "to go into law," or "to go into medicine,"—or to "go into" something other than industry. Yet, from the time of Eli Whitney, the great U.S. economic machine was built because some of the very best and brightest people went into manufacturing, marketing, personnel—the trenches where the economic battle is fought. U.S. executives have become increasingly preoccupied with corporate shells, with mergers and acquisitions.

On whose behalf is all of the merger and acquisition activity undertaken? The stockholders are worse off. My colleague, William Fruhan, did a comprehensive study that showed that it is not advisable to buy into a diversified conglomerate, if an investor wants to diversify a portfolio. The investor will be much better off, the data show in detail, to diversify that portfolio by buying stock in firms in an appropriate range of industries.[2]

And what happens in an organization that has been merged into another? People update their resumes. The talk is all about what the new policies are going to be, what the new jobs are going to be. Productivity is virtually neutralized as the organization changes hands. We have spent 10 to 20 years in swapping the assets of U.S. companies, essentially degrading their quality with each swap. That has been done at great cost to the economy. And it has been done because, I think, the business people at the top want quick results.

These are some of the reasons why we have not forcefully integrated technology and manufacturing into corporate strategies. But such integration should have at least as much weight as what is to be done in finance, or what will be done with retained earnings, or how the P/E ratio is to be increased.

By the way, we are never going to exceed or even catch the Japanese in quality. We may come close; indeed, we have in many cases. But we shall never succeed in using quality as a competitive weapon. And our days of being the lowest-cost producer in the world appear to be numbered.

Our great and bright hope for competitive advantage probably lies in the adroit use of our technology. But to do that we must do a much better job than we did in consumer electronics.

The Automobile Industry

Let me turn to the automobile industry. The landed cost advantage of Japanese cars over U.S.-made cars ranges from $1,400 to roughly $1,600 per car, of which employee cost is the largest component. The Japanese employee cost advantage is about $1,200. Some of this is accounted for by a $10 per-hour wage differential between: $20 a

delivered hour (i.e., an hour actually worked) in Detroit, about $10 in Japan. But the important factor in the labor differential is that the Japanese use about a third to 40 percent the number of workers to produce a car than we do. That advantage is also reflected in the cost of components from suppliers, a $700 advantage. And Japanese capital costs are lower ($146 per car). They tend to have less inventory, and their plants are, as a rule, smaller and more efficiently laid out. The Japanese pay $400 to ship the car across the Pacific, but have a net advantage of about $1,500.

Clearly we have a terrible productivity problem. And the auto industry is not alone. Most mechanically based industries, most smokestack industries, are in roughly the same shape. They use one-half to two-thirds more workers than the Japanese do per unit of product. Even firms that have successfully repelled the Japanese invasion, like Black and Decker, still face the same labor productivity differential. It is a U.S., and probably a Western European, disease. It is not something found exclusively in Detroit.

Here is a comparison with a moral: I visited the Kamigo Engine Plant, in Toya City, Japan, that had been in operation since the early 1960's. The plant was very efficient. It turned out little four-cylinder engines for Toyota very efficiently, and it took about three hours of labor to make an engine. Subsequently—this was about 1980—I visited a brand new engine plant in Detroit. It had the latest technology. It had cylinder heads with automatic rejection of defective ones. It had double-feedback controls on the machine-tool cutting surfaces. It had computerized hot-charge testing of engines. The equipment had been brought from Japan, Germany and the United States, and represented the state of the art in machine tools—but the labor content was six hours an engine.

We talk a lot about U.S. plants being too old; about our real need for more technology. Yet the most highly automated engine plant in the world was using twice as much labor per unit of output as a Japanese plant that was based on 15-year-old technology. The point is that many people have claimed that we can buy our way out of the productivity problem, that all we have to do is invest in more CAD/CAM, or in more robots. We have advanced the bombed-out hypothesis: The Japanese have an advantage because we blew up their plants and they have new ones. This pair of examples surely challenges these views.

Why the Japanese advantage? One reason is better process yield. The Japanese lines were up and running perhaps 99 percent of the time. In Detroit, the typical figure is 75 percent. More often than not, the Japanese product quality was higher, and so there was less rework.

In Japan, when the production line goes down, what happens next resembles a triple play in baseball. One worker is under the equipment repairing it. The foreman

[2]William E. Fruhan, *Financial Strategy: Studies in the Creation, Transfer, and Destruction of Shareholder Value.* Homewood, Ill.: Richard D. Irwin, 1979.

is setting up the line, and another worker is clearing away the debris. The line is up and running again very quickly. When a line is down in a U.S. plant, there is likely to be a jurisdictional dispute between the steamfitters and the electricians about who is to repair it. And if the foreman so much as lays his hands on the broken parts, he is cited for an unfair labor practice.

Although they had failures in the old engine plant, the Japanese were able to keep the machines up and running because of the devotion of the workers, how they had been trained, and the extensive cooperation between foremen and other levels of management. Workers felt proud of their equipment and their jobs. They did not feel that they were mere appendages to machines. Rather, they felt that the machines were theirs, and that it was their responsibility to make the machines run right.

A second reason for this two-to-one labor productivity difference is absenteeism—10 percent here; 1 percent in Japan. A third reason is the number of job categories: nearly 100 or so in Detroit; very few in Japan. The Japanese have flexible interchange of jobs.

The fourth reason is quality. As a rule, the Japanese do not use incoming quality inspection. They expect to get materials and supplies free of defects. We asked one Japanese supplier if it had ever shut down Toyota's main line. The answer: "Four years ago, on a Tuesday at 8:30 a.m., we shut Toyota down for 18 minutes, and we received lots of technical assistance from Toyota after that. Toyota engineers flocked in and they made sure that we did not have that kind of problem again." The Japanese have highly cooperative relationships between the suppliers and the manufacturers.

To sum up, the causes of our problem of unfavorable labor productivity are people causes. We are mistaken if we think that we are going to solve the problem by installing robots. What that will probably do is make the problem worse, because the more machines that are connected in tandem on a production line, the more likely it is to fail. On the other hand, one gains an advantage with a work force that can repair the line quickly. Take Toyo Kogyo, which in the early 1970's made the Mazda with the rotary Wankel engine. The firm was doing very well. Mazda's U.S. sales went from 48,000 in 1971 to 170,000 in 1972, and 186,000 in 1973. The labor content of the cars was very high, about at the U.S. level: 91 to 106 hours per car, depending on the year.

Toyo Kogyo is a really interesting example because it is a high-technology Japanese automobile company. It was the first to use robots. It was the first to use computers. It decided it needed a high-technology engine in order to break into the world market, which it did successfully. Then the EPA accused Mazda of being a gas-guzzler. Indeed, Mazda had the worst fuel-consumption ratings. And its U.S. sales went from 186,000 in 1973 to 164,000 in 1974 to 93,000 in 1978.

Matters were chaotic. The inventory went through the roof and Sumitomo Bank was about to come into provide "technical assistance," which meant telling Toyo Kogyo what it could do with its assets. And the Japanese press crowed: "A dead company." At that point there was a debate within the company as to whether to adopt the U.S. model and use more computers and more inventory control, or to pursue the Japanese approach.

The decision was made—I am sure with the assistance of Sumitomo—that the company would adopt the Toyota system. The results were absolutely startling. In five years, the direct labor content per car went from 96 hours to 43 hours. The sales penetration in the United States went from 146,000 to 299,300 units per year in 1980. As a result when Toyo Kogyo had more workers than it needed, it put ties on the redundant employees and told them: "If you believe in lifetime employment, go out and sell a car to your uncle, to your cousin, or to your mother, but get off the shop floor so that you don't clutter up the place."

A dramatic story, reducing the labor content by over 50 percent in five years, and in a company as vertically integrated as Ford. Spectacular results came from putting in a new system of management. What were its salient features?

The first thing emphasized was inventory. The Japanese view of inventory and the U.S. view of it are entirely different, as everyone knows. The Japanese think of inventory as water in a channel, with ships sailing on it. There are coral rocks at the bottom of the channel. Our solution would be to raise the water level so as not to worry about the rocks. Their solution is to lower the water level, cut up the rocks, lower the water level some more, cut up some more rocks, until inventory amounts to an almost continuous flow process.

The Japanese have a just-in-time inventory system; we have a just-in-case system. We keep extra inventory around, just in case something fails or the shipments do not arrive. But their system really puts stress on the organization. It makes middle management work hard. It makes the workers fret, because problems with defective materials and parts arise. But defective materials and parts do not pile up, and quality feedback is immediate.

An experienced observer of the U.S. labor scene might say: "If you did that to an American worker, he'd give you the bird.'I'm not going to work that much harder for no more pay if you lower the inventory level like that and force me to solve those problems and to fix things up at the same time I'm putting out good products.'"

Certainly the Japanese approach does cause stress. It is like pulling a chain till the weakest link breaks—unless there is an organized work system. And, of course, this is the real key to Japanese management, and it is the key to good U.S. management as well. Most of our renascent firms—GE, Ford, General Motors, Black and Decker, Cummings Engine, Deere—have instituted work practices that tend to be similar in some respects to the Japanese.

The Seven Pillars of Japanese Management

Here are some significant characteristics found in many Japanese companies.

(1) The corporate family concept. Sony's manager in San Diego talks about his family of American workers: My suppliers, my customers, my stockholders, my employees. We're all in the same family. We have to take care of each other. One consequence of this concept is that Japanese firms tend to stick with the same suppliers over time, rather than choosing them on the basis of competitive bidding.

The security of lifetime employment is part of the family concept. So are company-sponsored housing, recreational facilities, and discount stores.

Workers perceive that they are all part of the same organization. Sony, for example, insists that managers meet at least once a month with every employee in the firm in groups no larger than 40.

(2) No status symbols. There are virtually no symbols of status difference—no executive parking lot, no executive dining room; no fancy offices for senior executives. Workers and managers are virtually indistinguishable in dress. Most U.S. firms, by contrast, reek with status symbols.

(3) Job enrichment by vertical enlargement. For 20 years, we have managed on the assumption that the way to build worker satisfaction was to integrate the job horizontally. To put it a bit cynically, "horizontal enlargement" is the belief that a meaningful job results from adding up 150 "Mickey Mouse" jobs.

The Japanese, on the other hand, have enlarged their jobs vertically. Workers have responsibility for maintenance of their machines. The workers "own" the machines. They have to make the machines work well. They are proud of the machines. Every worker group I have seen in Japan does industrial engineering, for which it has been trained, in terms of its own methods and standards and procedures. Thus the group has a planning responsibility.

(4) The workers' on-the-job performance is made highly visible. At Honda, I saw workers screwing on taillights. They were carrying taillights to the work station one at a time. I was bewildered. Would not it have made sense to put a little hook on the lights so that they could be carried ten at a time? Just-in-time inventory is fine, but this manifestation seemed extreme. My guide said: "We want this task to be highly visible. We don't want any bends in the way because if this worker fails, we want everyone to see. We want everyone to be aware, particularly with tight inventories, that this is the one who shut down the line." Peer pressure was clearly used as a whip in that plant. But the visibility of the job is employed positively as well as negatively. There are awards and ceremonies for good performance and outstanding work.

(5) Harmonized values of workers and union leaders. One out of every four Japanese CEO's has been a union leader. I asked some young Japanese executives what they would do to get ahead. One answer was: "One thing is to become liked by our fellow workers and get elected union president, which means quitting the company. Then, after a couple of years, come back as a company officer." Union leadership training is considered vitally important by the Japanese management structure. If our managers had been union members or union officers at some point, wouldn't they have an easier relationship with unions?

(6) Managed group activities, which is what I call quality circles.

(7) Lots of training in how to do the job. Training decreases boredom by giving the worker the sense of prestige and knowledge. Japanese emphasize things like quality control, partly because it is intrinsically important and partly because it is the language the management and the workers speak in common. They can talk about quality control with no status differences.

Most Japanese firms do not institute all these approaches simultaneously. The point in detailing them is that we think that U.S. workers are not going to put up with any of this. They are not going to subjugate themselves to their jobs the way that Japanese workers do.

Studies have shown that in ranking their personal allegiances Japanese managers list company, self, family, or company, family, self, in one of those orders. U.S. and Western European managers almost all list self, family and company—in that order. What this means is that we are not going to get the same dedication to the company the Japanese have. This underscores the magnitude of our quality and productivity problems.

We are closing the gap on our disadvantages. We are introducing some changes and we could introduce some better ones. Nucor Steel, a small steel company, is competing successfully with the Japanese. It has lower cost than its Japanese competitors and is taking market share away from them. Nucor's management is using its workers as a competitive weapon. Its light truck business is taking market share back from the Japanese in a market they created. U.S. plants in that company are run with quality workers and they make quality products. The managements of these companies recognize that there cannot be quality products without a quality work force.

We must use the management of technology as the ultimate competitive weapon, instead of relying, as we traditionally have, on our ability to be the low-cost producers. But that change will require some important management changes in terms of management structure, in top management, and in the way we deal with people.

Simple Steps for Improving
Productivity and Competitiveness
James E. Ashton

I think it is unlikely that automation is a magic solution; that if we would just embrace the new technology of integration and automation and get the new technology on our factory floors, that would solve our problems of productivity and international competition. Not only is that unlikely to be the answer, but, more generally, I do not think there is a single answer.

To offer an anecdote about shipbuilding. I spent a time in the submarine business, and tried to understand why U.S. shipbuilders are second-rate, if I am generous, compared with the Japanese. A Japanese professor has written a fairly brief, but reasonably thorough, history of Japanese shipbuilding from the end of world War II until the mid-1970's. In that interval, the Japanese evolved from being essentially equal to the United States, in terms of manhours for building equivalent ships, to building ships for 40 percent of the manhours required to build them in this country. That represents a fairly impressive competitive change over two or three decades. What impresses the reader of the history is what the Japanese did not do. They did not invest vast amounts of capital; in fact, in the 1960's and early 1970's, more capital was spent in U.S. shipyards than in theirs. They did not bring striking new technology into their yards. They did nothing startling—but everything they did produced positive change.

They changed the general layout of the shipyards and the work structure. They stopped on-board construction after they had the hull put together, and installed the rest of the ship in packages which were assembled "off-hull." They broke those packages down into little work groups, and managed those groups well. The result was that in the 1970's the Japanese built 70 percent of the commercial ships in the world. The United States now captures zero percent of the competitive commercial shipbuilding in the world. The only commercial shipbuilding we do is mandated by law, or involves ships destined only for service on inland waters. What the Japanese did was not magical: They continuously changed things, and always for the better.

The Federal Government's Role

Several contributors discussed the role of government vis-a-vis such issues as international competition, investment, productivity, quality and the stimulation of new technology through the defense and space programs.

Hayward Thomas: There should, there must, be incentives to invest to modernize our plants. I think there is another role for government. It was proven before the Trade Commission in 1978 that the Japanese used tactics that are illegal in this country in the motorcycle market, yet the government took no action. The United States certainly cannot survive as a manufacturing country if we allow other countries to employ tactics that are not consistent with our laws to capture our markets. And we cannot trade with our trading partners who do not permit our products to enter their markets. I think the European Economic Community is taking a much more realistic stand on this.

I do not believe I am a protectionist, but we must have equitable trade. We cannot have free trade and survive as a manufacturing country if anybody can dump products into our markets, using undervalued currency, government subsidies, and things of that kind.

It is government's role to maintain a fair competitive posture. If the government is going to protect us, we in industry must make the necessary investments to continue in business. The government cannot be expected to bail us out when we have a problem.

Thomas J. Murrin: In those industrial areas where we directly face Japanese competition, unless the government becomes much more significantly and supportively involved, very few of our present companies will, in my judgment, prevail competitively over the long run. There are a lot of things the Federal Government can do—and should be doing—right now. One example is its efforts in manufacturing technology and technology modernization that are beginning to provide extraordinary stimulation to the U.S. aerospace and defense industries. These efforts will provide the government and the citizens with better products at lower cost. The government should be doing much more of this sort of thing.

Thomas L. Skelly: Xerox is getting some benefit from the new microelectronics VLSI (Very Large-Scale Integration) program, which the government is underwriting fairly heavily to make sure that it protects special-purpose microelectronics for future military systems. But the investment is not all made by the government. We are probably putting $100 million into R&D and new facilities for related programs. This is a good example of how a little up-front subsidy can make sure that U.S. industry maintains its lead in certain types of electronics.

Harry B. Thompson: Although the results of the government programs may not have been all we thought they might be, they have been positive. Unfortunately, I do not think that the results have been well transferred, even to defense-related companies. And my experience with nondefense related companies is that they simply do not understand what the programs are and their significance for industry.

Stephen R. Rosenthal: My preliminary research shows that the government's defense-related promotion of advanced manufacturing technology is not of much benefit to smaller companies. This should be further investigated. If this proves to be the case, reasons should be identified and implications should be addressed as a matter of public policy.

Robert J. Mayer: I think the Federal Government is beginning to play a more effective role in providing incentives for investment and other programs of the sort it has provided to the aerospace and defense industries. Legislation is needed to provide additional incentives in the form of tax credits to encourage investment. Granting such incentives is a rightful role for government.

James A. Baker: The big issue to me, and I think to General Electric, is interest rates. Somehow we have to get interest rates in the United States competitive with rates in other countries. Another problem is the support of exports. No country, particularly no major industrialized country, should subsidize exports—but they do and we compete against them. This is where the government can help. I think we have the money to invest or can get it; I think industry has the technology or can get that.

Joel D. Goldhar: The best single thing the Federal Government could do would be to tell everybody that there are not going to be solutions in Washington to problems that start in company boardrooms. And whatever public policies and incentives and tax programs are adopted, stability is probably more important than their exact form, so that industry can have a long enough time horizon for strategic planning.

Part III
What Corporate Management Must Understand—and Do

Automate, Emigrate or Evaporate
James A. Baker

U.S. industry faces three choices in the 1980's: automate, emigrate or evaporate. Each of these choices is unpopular in some circles. But the choice must be made nonetheless—and the buck stops in the corporate office. That is where the decision is made to abandon the business or to take measures to save it. Automation is seen as a threat to jobs in some industries. It may well pose a threat to *some* jobs in *some* industries. But the alternatives to automation are (1) the loss of *all* jobs, as companies die, or (2) moving offshore.

We are competing against hourly labor rates of $2.15 in Mexico, $1.38 in Singapore, 76 cents in India. Compare those with the $8-to-$15 rates in Kentucky or Indiana. Even automation is not enough to keep some extremely labor-intensive businesses in the United States. GE makes all its radios and tapes recorders offshore because we have not yet devised a way to make them here and compete in price against manufacturers from the Far East. In fact, even the Japanese are moving radio and tape production from their shores, looking for cheaper labor rates. A global migration of labor-intensive industries is in progress.

The world economic situation has changed drastically in the past two decades. Third World countries, especially the non-oil-producing ones, are facing massive debts because they must import their energy and most of their manufactured goods. Labor-intensive manufacturing is one way they can earn revenue and, perhaps, avoid bankruptcy. I would submit that exporting very low-technology jobs to those countries is not only good for them, but is in our own eventual best interest, if they can be kept solvent and remain customers for U.S. products.

This country *cannot* afford to turn its back on—to wash its hands of—the key lunch-pail industries that its population centers depend upon, and go running off looking for a golden future in services or "pure high tech." The technology to make U.S. industries world-competitive once again is not somewhere off the horizon. It has been *here* for years. We *invented* most of it. But we have to make the decision to *use* it. No industry, no matter how primitive or mature, is immune to improvement from technology.

The Corporate Transition to Superior Manufacturing Performance
James F. Lardner

Faced with increasingly successful offshore competition and sharp declines in shares of world markets, U.S. managers are beginning to look hard at the need to achieve superior manufacturing performance to guarantee survival. This management concern represents an important change from a few years ago, when U.S. companies dominated the world market for manufactured goods. For over 20 years, from the early 1950's until the latter half of the 1970's, there was little reason to believe that U.S. factories did not represent a standard of manufacturing performance unequaled anywhere in the world.

Events of the past several years have shaken that belief, however. We in the United States now are struggling to establish standards by which superior manufacturing performance can be measured in world global competition. Based on what we are learning from the new group of competitors we are facing, I am convinced that many of the measurements we have used to judge manufacturing performance in the past 30 years will need to be altered or, perhaps, even abandoned entirely. This will not be an easy task; after so many years of comfortable, unchallenged domination of world markets, the U.S. industrial culture will not take kindly to change.

Characteristics of Superior Performance

To define what I think are now the marks of superior manufacturing performance:

• For a given output, superior manufacturing performance will permit significant reduction in plant size. Savings of a third to a half in total facility size will be comfortably possible.

• For a given output, superior manufacturing performance will require far fewer people. The principal areas of reduction will be in indirect and white-collar workers, who so far have been viewed as the beneficiaries of the transition to the factory of the future.

• Factories capable of superior manufacturing performance will operate with minimal inventories, and will be notable for high throughput velocity. Manufacturing quality will be high; defective material and work will approach zero; postproduction costs—primarily warranties due to manufacturing defects—will be lower.

• Factories capable of superior manufacturing performance will demonstrate great flexibility in responding to changes in schedule and in product mix. These factories will be capable of rapid start-up at much lower cost when beginning to make new or revised products.

• Products will be manufactured in these factories at substantially lower unit costs, offering greater value for the money to the customer: an important advantage in a world of global competition.

For several years, Deere & Company has been engaged in the corporate effort directed to achieving superior manufacturing performance in its industry. So far, progress has been encouraging and we are optimistic about the future. We still have a long way to go to reach the goals we have set, but we have learned much from our own experience. We have also learned a great deal from companies that have come to see what we are doing and from visits to companies engaged in similar programs. We can now begin to identify some of the important elements we think must be present if any program to achieve superior manufacturing performance is to succeed.

Necessary Elements for Success

The first, and perhaps most important, factor is the environment in which the effort is to take place. There are two conditions which, I believe, must exist. First, there must be a visible, top-down commitment to the program by senior management. Although it is not reasonable to expect that members of this group will (or

should) become involved in every detail, it is essential that they understand the strategic implications of the undertaking. They must insist on an overall plan that will ensure that there is a broadly distributed, well-coordinated introduction of the technologies and the organizational changes that will be required to achieve success. They must also ensure that adequate resources are available for a sufficient length of time to get the job done. Achieving superior manufacturing performance is not a short-term project.

The second critical factor is how a majority of the existing management group use manufacturing. Currently, there are two distinct views of the nature of manufacturing itself. The first, which has its intellectual and philosophical roots in Frederick Taylor's principles of scientific management and the specialization that resulted from those principles, holds that manufacturing can be divided into a series of small, easily definable elements according to established specialities within the manufacturing spectrum. Advocates of this view believe that if each of these separate elements is optimized, the whole manufacturing operation will automatically be optimized also. This is the approach we have been following for the last 30 or 40 years, and it has produced the kinds of manufacturing facilities and the organizations that we have today.

There is, however, a new school or, perhaps I should say, a revisionist school, that views manufacturing as a single, indivisible whole that includes much more than the material transformation activity commonly thought of as manufacturing. This school holds that manufacturing begins with product concept and design and ends with service of the product in the field. Further, though manufacturing is infinitely complex in all of its multitude of fine details, no single part can be treated in isolation from all other parts. This view of manufacturing is driving current efforts to integrate CAD and CAM, and it is the concept that is behind programs to achieve computer-integrated manufacturing, which is expected to be the foundation for the true factory of the future. It also seems to be close to the view held by the Japanese, which has led them to just-in-time manufacturing, the integration of material handling into manufacturing operations, the successful pursuit of quality, and the integration of design and manufacturing activities, which results in cost-effective manufactured products.

The idea that the task of optimizing manufacturing must be approached in an overall manner is not appealing to many operating managers and members of existing staff groups. In fact, two of the most important staff departments, industrial engineering and cost accounting, have been instrumental in developing many of the measurement standards for manufacturing performance we use today, and they will not easily be persuaded to change.

Nevertheless, if there is not a fairly broadly distributed

recognition of the indivisible nature of manufacturing by the management group, it will be impossible to establish a successful program to achieve superior manufacturing performance. Our own experience, and the experience of others to date, argues that a fractionalized approach simply will not work.

People are next on the list of requirements for success. Achievement of superior manufacturing performance demands a special mix of people in the management and the staff groups, a mix not always found in manufacturing operations. It is my belief that if this mix does not exist, it must be created. My ideal group of people would be something close to the following: First, there must be an adequate number of truly competent, experienced manufacturing managers and senior technical specialists, who have thought carefully about the way we presently look at and manage manufacturing, and who are constructively dissatisfied with the results. Second, there must be a group of engineers and technicians trained in the use of computer-based technology and systems and capable of applying these skills to solving practical problems. This group should be made up of the younger people who lack the depth of experience in operations and the judgment such experience brings. The third group will be the outside consultants who will be needed in a few highly specialized areas. Finally, and perhaps most important, it is essential that there be some people with broad experience in high-level manufacturing management and problems of technology transfer to provide the intellectual leadership required in these new and unchartered waters.

There is no formula for the exact mix of experience, skill and talent, since it will depend to a degree on the specific situation. I think it is safe to say, however, that most early estimates of the amount of resources required are optimistic. So be prepared to search these people out and to evaluate their capabilities well before they are needed.

From my own experience, I would say the most difficult resources to find are the senior-level, broad-gauged people who can provide the intellectual leadership for the program. Only slightly less difficult to find are the experienced middle-level management and senior technicians who have come to question the assumptions upon which the present approaches to manufacturing management and manufacturing control are based, and who are convinced that there is a better way to do things.

In addition to creating the environment and finding the right people, it is essential to define the program itself. It is likely that, at least at the beginning, the program definition will not be detailed. In the early stages, no one is sure exactly what needs to be done to get from here to there. The plan then must depend heavily on basic concepts for setting goals and directions. A good starting point is to decide what results are expected and to work back from there.

Deere's Experience

When we began our program, we had not defined the characteristics of superior manufacturing performance nearly as clearly as I have defined them above. We did have a pretty good idea, though, that the kind of factory these characteristics describe was a good example of what we wanted to achieve. From that start the collective judgment of the project's two senior groups focused on a strategy that was later found to be very successful. A review of the objectives of the program set by the groups led to an important conclusion: If the goals could be achieved, some very substantial reductions in total cost of manufacture would result. We decided, therefore, that if we could identify the major influences on manufacturing costs, we could also identify the sources of the principal problems standing between us and the achievement of superior manufacturing performance.

For some time, a number of the most experienced people involved in our program had suspected that the rapid growth of manufacturing overhead accounts and manufacturing costs was not simply the result of the increasing complexity of the manufacturing operation itself. Rather, they believed this growth was caused in large part by our failure to respond effectively to the changed environment. Our problem, however, was that the objectives of the program to achieve superior manufacturing performance had been defined by people who took a holistic view of manufacturing, while the financial and operational control and reporting systems available to measure progress were designed to deal only with the many small pieces that resulted from using the conventional fractionalized approach to manufacturing. Thus, in estimating the possible effects of changes we were contemplating when we tried to establish baseline cost data from which to work, we found that the cost trends frequently became lost in the wilderness of the overhead accounts. This was particularly true of the fixed overhead categories, where the link between overhead costs and the actual causes of those costs was tenuous or nonexistent.

We decided that to get a realistic estimate of the likely results, we needed a means of cost analysis that would give us a base from which to evaluate the proposals developed in the project. It was clear that we needed a way of looking at the whole manufacturing activity if we could. To this end we turned to a simplified version of value analysis. That step took us from minute details to the overall view in one great jump; it did give us the beginning of the insight we were seeking.

We began with total factory selling price, which was then divided into three parts: direct material, defined as all material, in whatever form, purchased to become part of the finished product; transformation costs, defined as all costs related to transforming the direct material into the end product; and margin, which obviously was the difference between factory selling price and the sum of direct material plus transformation costs. Value Added then became Transformation Costs plus Margin, a relatively simple concept.

Although we recognized that the cost of direct material was influenced by product design and we considered that product design was logically an important factor in achieving superior manufacturing performance, we decided to treat it as a longer-term problem, which we could address after we had examined transformation costs. Because material transformation is commonly thought of as the manufacturing operation, that seemed a good place to start.

As we examined this breakdown in more detail, we began to learn where the problems were and why we had them. Although the conclusions derived from this exercise have not been universally accepted throughout the organization, they are increasingly held by key manufacturing executives and operational managers. It was the analysis of the transformation costs that gave us our first real clue as to what the problems might be. While it is possible to divide transformation costs into a very large number of classifications, we chose to keep the exercise as simple as possible and still identify the origins of the costs involved in actually making the product.

We started with the following breakdown:

• Total employment costs for salaried employees, including fringe benefits: what it cost to keep those people on the payroll.
• Total employment costs for indirect labor in the blue-collar group.
• Total employment costs for direct labor in the blue-collar group.

For the first time we had broken fringe benefits out of the overhead accounts and so had an idea of true employment costs.

We then set up a classification of material-transformation costs other than employment costs; we chose to call this simply nonemployment costs. Because some senior managers were convinced we had serious problems with energy, depreciation and interest costs, we broke out these nonemployment costs separately. We also identified indirect materials and service costs, returns and allowances, and all other charges and credits, including the sales incentives and bonuses that are charged to the factories in our company.

After these breakdowns were completed we analyzed the trends in each category over the past 15 to 18 years. The conclusions were illuminating. The direct labor costs that we could relate to the physical transformation of material made up only a small portion of the total cost being charged to the transformation activity. In addition, there had been a relative reduction in these costs as a percentage of all costs associated with the transformation process. During the period, however, there had been a remarkable growth in the cost of salaried employment per unit of output and in nonemployment costs per unit of output, and a somewhat smaller—but still important—growth in indirect labor costs per unit of output. This was not what we had expected to discover, though there were some manufacturing managers who had suspected that this was, indeed, the reality. The next step was to find out why.

We began by assuming that everyone on the payroll was there because someone in management thought there was a job to be done. We also assumed that most people were working with due diligence and effort. The question to be answered, then, was: What caused all the extra work that these people were doing? It was in pursuit of this answer that we finally hit pay dirt. We analyzed what people were doing and how the money they were spending for nonemployment purposes was being allocated.

The increase in workloads, reflected in salaries and indirect costs, appeared at first to be the result of a tremendous increase in the essential complexity of manufacturing over the period studied. We estimated that it was about one order of magnitude greater than it had been 15 years earlier. But some people said this conclusion seemed too simple and raised two important questions.

The first was: How much of the increase in complexity really was unavoidable? The second was: How much of this problem was the result of the way we were dealing with the new manufacturing environment?

In considering the second question, the possibility that we might be needlessly compounding our problems struck some people as unlikely, but the more we thought about it, the more merit that question had. It was decided to investigate this possibility. I will not dwell on the details of how we tracked down the causes of unnecessary manufacturing complexity. Suffice it to say that the worst suspicions of those who had raised the question originally were confirmed. In pursuing the divide and optimize theory, we had completely lost sight of our basic manufacturing mission. For example, we had succeeded in separating design and manufacturing to the point where we had obscured the bedrock principle that we not only needed a product that performed satisfactorily and had features the customer wanted, but we also had to make it at a profit and be able to service it satisfactorily in the field.

Our typical introduction of new products was a sequential process: First, they were completely designed, then the manufacturing plan was prepared, the tooling and equipment were procured, the product was produced and sold and serviced. The result of this sequential approach was that tooling costs exceeded estimates; product introduction was late; or, if the target date was met, it was only with extra cost and effort. Product launches were followed by volumes of engineering changes needed by the shop for reasons of manufacturability. Start-up, scrap and rework all were customarily excessive. On the shop floor we had also pursued the philosophy of specialization. The majority of our departments were organized by machine-tool function, not by parts to be produced. This had the effect of dividing the material-transformation process on most production parts among so many people and departments that no one felt responsible for the end result. Further, by doing a small part of the total transformation in each of several departments, we greatly compounded the problem of production control and scheduling and increased material-handling costs enormously.

We also discovered, as we analyzed the physical attributes of the parts we were making, that we could identify repeated patterns of similar geometric and physical characteristics common to a number of parts. This, of course, led us to Group Technology and part-classification coding, which we now use to identify families of parts and to select and lay out machinery and equipment to form manufacturing units to produce those families. The results of the use of Group Technology concepts have been rewarding. We have reduced costs, increased throughput, improved quality, reduced response time, and, most important, we have started to return responsibility for operations to the shop floor, which makes it possible to simplify the production control and scheduling problems. As we look back, we can see now what we should have recognized before. If a factory has 10,000 parts and is making them 10,000 different ways, there will be far greater management and control problems than if 20-part families can be identified in those 10,000 parts, and they can be made in only 500 different ways. These changes were also reflected in a decrease in the number of overhead personnel involved in support of the transformation process. When we looked at what most of them were doing, we found the majority were engaged in data and information processing. Therefore, with the complexity of the operation reduced, the data generated are reduced and fewer people are needed. Simplification also allows greater use of computers to do much of the work formerly done by overhead people. It is unfortunate, but true, that most of the work those people were doing was routine, involving highly structured repetitive decision making. In that environment computers almost always do a faster, more accurate job, leading to important reductions in costly errors and omissions.

Lessons Learned

We believe that the road to superior manufacturing performance does not begin with large capital investment programs. Nor does the road begin with the wholesale adoption of new and exotic technologies. It really starts with an examination of the total manufacturing operation and with a program to reduce these operations to human dimensions by reintegrating them into a comprehensible, manageable whole.

In our company, we are now beginning to measure the results of programs to reintegrate manufacturing. Little by little, we are picking up the fractured pieces and putting them back together. We finally have design and manufacturing engineers working as teams to produce manufacturable designs the first time. We have seen tooling costs cut in half, and we have seen reductions in manufacturing costs of 10 to 20 percent.

We have rearranged large portions of our factories to make it possible to establish flow-through manufacturing. Our savings have reached into all phases of the transformation operation: material handling, reduced 40 percent; utilization, up 15 percent; throughput, up 15 percent; defective material and work, down 50 percent. These are satisfying results. We have also begun to welcome workers back into the decision-making group from which scientific management ejected them years ago.

In summary, we are working hard to simplify the total manufacturing problem by pulling together the pieces that have been so carefully separated over the past 40 years. There are no miracles. There is only hard work. It has been a long time since our quality has been as high, our overall efficiency as good, and our management as able to manage effectively. We believe that we are indeed on the road to superior manufacturing performance.

Top Management's Role: The Invisible Software
Harry B. Thompson

What *excites* me about advanced manufacturing technology and its software is the rewarding possibilities they afford us. What *concerns* me is the will of U.S. industry to step up to the challenges and the opportunities of new computer integrated manufacturing. In my view, management must take the lead by becoming the software that will pull everything together and move U.S. industry into a new era of competitiveness.

Three things stand out about this technology:

(1) Adoption of advanced process technology is essential if much of this country's manufacturing base is going to become competitive again.

(2) Process technology is more than a manufacturing issue. Because of its strategic implications and its pervasiveness in the business, it is now a business issue that must be dealt with by top management.

(3) Technology cannot be treated in a vacuum. It affects every function, every activity of business operations.

There is much interest in manufacturing technology and what it might do for us. There is hardly an issue of any business or major trade journal that goes by without some reference to these subjects. In the consulting business itself, we see new or renewed interest on the part of CEO's. At Kearney, we recently held three briefings on smokestack industry for CEO's in the Chicago area. Each briefing sold out. If we had done that two, three, four or five years ago, no one would have attended those meetings.

There seems to be genuine interest. But there has been very little action; certainly not enough.

Even those companies that have begun to meet the challenge of manufacturing technology are simply installing islands of automation, sophisticated process technologies, in the middle of a sea of old, conventional, standard, 1950's-type equipment. There is nothing intrinsically wrong with islands of automation (see below, page 22). But they are far removed from the computer-integrated factory of the future that we read so much about. Much of the technology application thus far has taken place in the metal-working companies that have significant fabrication and machining activities. The potential for some of the more sophisticated assembly operations is increasing daily, however, as more versatile robotics and other devices are coming on the scene.

Why is industry so slow to adopt this new technology? In our studies, in our visits with clients over the past two or three years, we have observed two broad reasons for this: (1) internal conditions in a company—cultural, structural, organizational and functional factors within a company, which inhibit the introduction of major change; and (2) external conditions, the broader environment in which we all live—the market, the government, the educational systems, and so forth. I would like to review these internal and external conditions and use them as the basis to set forth, in my view, what it is that the CEO's across the country must do to find out where technology fits into their organizations and how to move forward with the introduction of that technology.

Internal Conditions

There are three reasons (maybe they are excuses also) why managers do not do anything:

(1) A functional and parochial approach to management itself;

(2) The so-called investment barriers; and

(3) The potential implementation problems associated with massive programs and the massive change they entail.

A Functional and Parochial Approach to Management

Functional thinking and organization can prevent managers from seeing the full range of opportunities af-

forded by computer-integrated technology. Because of its flexibility, computerized process technology provides the potential for cost effectively introducing new products for both existing and new markets. As such, it becomes strategic: Its real value transcends manufacturing or any other manufacturing function. For this reason, managers must view process technology from a broad perspective.

Many CEO's have backgrounds in marketing, finance and law. While this is not necessarily bad, it does mean that many top managers do not have the background required to understand the significance of the new technology. Even worse, often they are not interested. Functional managers who do understand—and there are many—complain that they cannot get their bosses' attention. This condition often leads top management to view the new technology as a sophisticated cost reducer and not as a strategic weapon.

Many senior managers are taking a wait-and-see attitude. Some are not convinced their competition will invest, so they are reluctant to move ahead. Some believe they can let others do the groundwork and make the mistakes. Then they will implement changes with relative ease. Others fear obsolescence of the technology, which is changing rapidly.

In any case, this attitude indicates a failure to understand the cultural, structural and evolutionary change required to put the new technology in place. Companies such as Messerschmitt and Deere have spent up to seven years in bringing a flexible manufacturing system on stream. The internal environment must be changed to accept this radical departure from standard manufacturing practices. Even if a generic system were available, it could not be installed and operating effectively in a short period of time. The truth is that one just cannot wait without risking competitive suicide.

Also, it seems many top managers fail to recognize that competition may surface from new sources due to the flexibility of the new processes. For example, what would happen if Deere, with its flexible machining capabilities, started to make aircraft parts?

Finally, over the past 20 years, there has been a preoccupation with portfolio management, which tends to rearrange assets and make a company look better on paper. In reality, these activities do nothing to enhance the competitive position of this country and serve to distract us from the real job of increasing productivity. Robert Reich, in his book *The Next American Frontier* coins the term "paper entrepreneurialism" to describe this phenomenon.[1]

Many of the conditions described above are present due to a narrow, as opposed to strategic, view of manufacturing on the part of many CEO's.

[1]Robert B. Reich, *The Next American Frontier*. New York: Times Books, 1983.

Barriers to Investment

The second set of internal impediments to action center around investment barriers. This is perhaps the most-often mentioned reason for inaction.

The investment justification process that emphasizes discounted cash-flow analysis biases heavily against the kind of long-range investment required to install this technology. This is especially true in times of high interest rates. When the rate reaches 20 percent, justification is nearly impossible.

Perhaps even more important than the method of justification is that most managers take into account only cost reduction and do not consider the revenue-generation potential of low-cost flexibility through added market share. Even when they focus exclusively on costs, typically, all costs are not considered. Seldom, for instance, is the cost of not doing something right the first time included. Often, reduced inventory and space costs are not included.

Much is made of risk analysis these days. Usually it is focused on the probability of a project failing and, therefore, further reduces the possibility of making long-term investments. Perhaps more important, but seldom considered, is the risk of not investing when others are doing so. The continued viability of the business may be at stake here.

Implementation Problems

The next internal area is fear of implementing these large programs, which are full of unknowns. It is difficult enough to implement small, localized projects utilizing conventional technology. In the case of computerized technology, major investments are required and implementation will affect every aspect of the business.

Specifically, management fears that the union and the workers will resist automation. The unions will likely be concerned that their importance may be diminished, while individual workers will fear for their jobs. They may both be right; however, inaction will be far worse in terms of job loss. *Some* business is better than *no* business. The human aspects of automation must be dealt with if the company is to become competitive. There are no easy answers.

Not only hourly labor, but also supervisors may feel threatened by the computer. An officer of a major Chicago company recently said that selling technological change to first-line management is the toughest job of all.

There will probably be an insufficient number of skilled employees to support computerized manufacturing. Management must ask these questions:

- Where will the workers come from?
- Who will train them?
- How will we retain this scarce resource once they are trained?

If the above problems are not enough, programs of this magnitude are often fraught with cost overruns.

External Barriers

The external world offers up another set of problems to a company. These include: a shifting manufacturing base; a lack of government policy; and the education and retraining network.

Shifting Manufacturing Base

It has been predicted that the manufacturing base will continue to shift from developed to developing nations—for example, from the United States and Japan to South Korea and Southeast Asia. This may be true; however, this view can lull us into thinking there is no need to invest in manufacturing because it is going away anyway.

Many believe the shift is caused by cheap labor only. The truth is that some very sophisticated processes are being installed—processes that can allow the developing nations to compete on a wide range of products. Exporting technology to a sophisticated Third World country that could become a competitor is dangerous. If nothing else, it will certainly retard process-technology development and implementation in the United States.

Government Policy

It can be stated with certainty that the government lacks a comprehensive policy toward technological development. One area in which the Federal Government has been active is in defense-related manufacturing activities. Tech Mod, Industrial Productivity Improvement (IPI) and, lately, the Industrial Modernization Incentive Program (IM-IP) are all designed to encourage investment in modernized facilities. Progress has been slow and steady, but transfer of the developing technology to the manufacturing community at large has been disappointing. However, much can be learned by those who care to dig into the volumes of information generated through these programs.

Many states are sponsoring manufacturing research and development programs. To date, most of these programs have been narrow in scope and fragmented.

The Education and Retraining Network

The education and retraining network is insufficient to support the country's needs. The primary and secondary school systems are not preparing technically competent students. To a large extent, this is because so few opt for teaching technology. There is more money elsewhere. In addition, few universities develop manufacturing engineers capable of dealing with computerized technology.

Finally, there is no national program for retraining. The problem is too big for companies and the government does not even seem to understand the problem.

A Program for Action

The opportunities for action are many, but the problems are not insignificant. Management must step up and be counted if real progress is to be made. The question becomes: How do we start? Before getting specific, one tempering comment should be made: Technology may not be the answer in every industry or for all processes. However, CEO's should not make this decision by default; it should be made based on fact. So what can be done?

In a program of this magnitude and complexity, it is essential that management demand that manufacturing technology be thoroughly understood and dealt with at all levels of the company. The multifunctional implications of the technology make it imperative that the program have an advocate at the top management level.

The top management team must be knowledgeable about computerized technology and understand its strategic implications. This can accomplished by (1) reading plenty of articles, particularly those of a not too technical nature; (2) listening to company employees; and (3) talking to outsiders, including suppliers, consultants, and academicians.

While it is learning, management should begin to organize itself to deal with computerized technologies as a business issue and not as a cost-reduction project. This can be done by establishing a technology function with access to the CEO. In some companies, it might make sense to include this function in the strategic planning group. This could also serve to bring manufacturing into the strategic planning process.

Next, a task force reporting to the technology function should be formed. This task force should consist of middle-level functional managers. In addition to fact-finding, the main function of the task force will be to bring new ideas to the surface and to foster understanding at all levels of the organization. After the organization is in place and the education process is underway, a market-oriented study should be conducted to determine where technology can provide a competitive advantage and how it might affect business strategy.

Once the technology leverage points have been determined, the next step—a very important one—is the establishment of an operation strategy. An operation strategy is a set of policies that guide manufacturing-operating decisions that support overall business objectives. These policies establish the directions in process technology, "make versus buy," resource deployment and management structure. These areas are interrelated and need to be thought through again when a new process technology program is contemplated.

Once the manufacturing direction has been established, the focus should shift from study to action. Two concurrent activities have been used as a successful implementation approach by many companies.

The first is identify a product or a process that clearly needs upgrading or modernizing. Institute an automation program for utilizing computerized technology. Develop an "island of automation." The knowledge and experience gained through this project will be invaluable in preparing for the future. One thing is certain: Past manufacturing experience is not sufficient to implement integrated systems; the problems are different and the impact is broader.

At the same time that the "island of automation" is being implemented, a long-range technology-introduction plan should be prepared. This plan should build on the knowledge being gained on the "island" project and should include:

* Implementation priorities.
* Approaches to functional integration.
* Technology-training programs.
* Human and union relations strategies.
* Economic justification parameters.

To help in clearing the inevitable justification hurdle, especially on the first project, consider treating it as an R&D effort as opposed to a productivity-improvement project. This will allow the payback requirements to be loosened. Perhaps a "slush fund" should be established on which the only payback expected in the beginning is knowledge.

The job facing U.S. industry is not easy, but the rewards can be great. The time for action is now. The program outlined above can work, but only if it is pursued vigorously by a dedicated top mangement team.

Capital and Financial Planning for Farsighted Strategies
George A. Harter

The United States is entering into a second industrial revolution, one involving a transition from outmoded manufacturing facilities to automated factories of the future. The required technology and most of the associated building blocks are now available, so that those in U.S. industry with the necessary courage and foresight can start making the change. The decision as to how, when, and even whether, to proceed with the resulting massive investment required must be made by the companies' top managements. The time to decide is now because many businesses operate in an increasingly competitive worldwide environment that demands that they either change or perish.

Planning the Change

The actual need for a factory of the future should first be confirmed by a comprehensive strategic-planning effort. The scope and nature of the required investment needs to be coupled closely with a total business strategy, bolstered by a thorough competitive analysis.

This type of investment affects almost all functions within an organization. In contrast to the acquisition of a single large new piece of equipment, we must now view the investment from a total system perspective. The costs associated with peripheral capabilities, software, and employee training frequently exceed the cost of the basic manufacturing equipment. Start-up expenses are often the major cause of negative cash flow over the early months, or even years, of the project. In many cases, developing a factory of the future may mean abandoning old plant sites and building completely new facilities. All of these considerations must be weighed carefully in developing the optimum long-term strategy.

Any decision to invest in a major new capability must be based on a reasonably accurate estimate of the timing of expenditures to determine the required cash flow. Most management teams still lack the experience or resources required to assess adequately the many peripheral costs associated with significant technological changes. Consultants and equipment suppliers will have to be deeply involved in defining the new system configuration and in charting the course for change. The most serious threats to ultimate success are (1) failure to consider all aspects of the required investment; and (2) failure to apply the necessary resources and management attention to implement the change.

Evaluating the Change

Most companies now use some form of discounted cash-flow analysis to aid in evaluating major new investments. Internal rate-of-return and present-value calculations are understood by all of today's business-school graduates, by most industrial engineers, and even by a few older, general management types.

Use of discounted cash-flow analysis has drawn some criticisms in recent times because of a perception that it is biased toward short-term results. Critics blame overemphasis on cash-flow analysis for the failure of U.S. industry to keep pace with its Japanese counterparts in modernizing factories. If this claim has merit, then it is essential to address that issue when considering the implications of a second industrial revolution. If the problem is real, much of the change envisioned by manufacturing strategists will not gain acceptance by top corporate management because of financial considerations.

I believe that there is some merit in the criticism. However, the problem is not with discounted cash flow as an analytical tool, but rather with how it is applied in many companies. Too often, it is not the analytical tool itself that has a short-term bias, but, rather, those who use it. In this context, the immortal words of Pogo

somehow seem appropriate: ''We have met the enemy, and he is us.''

Management can choose between two basic approaches in measuring the cash flowing from an investment. The first, and more commonly used, is to measure cash flow by considering only the incremental benefit of a capital investment, based largely on reduction of product costs. This approach assumes that competitive factors will not change significantly over the life of the investment, and generally ignores the synergistic benefits of the investment for other aspects of the business, such as product quality or performance.

The second and more logical approach is to measure cash flow by considering the difference in probable future financial results for the total business, both with and without the investment. Unlike the first approach, this method takes into account the influence of changing environmental conditions, and directs management attention toward safeguarding or improving the competitive position over an extended future period.

The first, narrow approach is insensitive to the possibility that lack of an investment for technological innovation, either in product design or in manufacturing processes, could, in the long run, lead to a noncompetitive position in the marketplace or even to complete loss of the business. It will, therefore, quite often, undervalue the true return of a strategic investment, or group of investments, vital for the long-term health of a business. For that reason alone, it is imperative that a broader approach be adopted when evaluating the type of investments under consideration.

There is one problem, however, with a broad, strategic approach to investment analysis: It depends on a good understanding of the market dynamics and competitive situation over the useful life of the investment. We must first consider what will happen to our competitive position and resulting financial performance if we fail to make the investment. Then we must assess the improvement in competitive position and resulting financial performance if we do make the investment. The difference in net cash flow between the two alternatives should provide a reasonably good basis for evaluating the long-term benefit. Even with a wide range of uncertainty in future market and competitive scenarios, management can rely on this approach for a good assessment of the true value of a major technological investment, such as a factory of the future.

One message heard more and more is that top management must be better informed and more involved in the technological changes occurring in our factories. I endorse that thought completely, and add another: Top management must also become better grounded in the financial analysis techniques used to make investment decisions. The choice of analytic approach, along with the underlying assumptions, plays a critical role in determining the attractiveness of one investment over another. We need to be sure that decisions about major technological advances are not viewed too narrowly, and that the projected return on investment is not grossly undervalued.

Financial Planning Considerations

To take a broader look at the situation, U.S. industry faces a massive problem of financing the technological changes discussed earlier. Each company must chart its own course for implementing the changes. That will involve not only identifying the obvious investment in new facilities and start-up operations, but also searching out peripheral, and sometimes obscure, costs. We will have to develop new management systems, acquire and train people, and phase out old manufacturing facilities. We will need to rationalize the proper and acceptable level of long-term investments against their impact on short-term financial performance.

It seems clear that most companies will have to approach this industrial-modernization problem both on a selective and on a time-phased basis. Limitations of financial and human resources will temper our ambitions to address all businesses and products with equal emphasis.

We will have to establish priorities relative to the attractiveness of alternative investments, of course, favoring those businesses and products that offer the best long-range return. To this end, the need for good, credible techniques of evaluating investment alternatives will be of critical importance.

One might question whether many U.S. companies will see the benefit of, or be able to afford, the sizable investments implied by a factory of the future. There are already many examples of such investments for a single, automated plant, but will this be practical for most businesses and products? The message of this report is that the investment in automation must be made to survive. But the question is: Will financial considerations force many businesses to make the hard choice of nonsurvival? This question will obviously have to be answered on a case-by-case basis, but perhaps we can gain some insight from current examples.

Most of the available examples are now provided by Japanese industry. Fanuc Ltd., in a plant near Mount Fuji, makes parts for robots and machine tools with automated machining centers that toil unattended throughout the night. The plant, with 54,000 square feet and an initial cost of about $32 million, has 30 machining cells, each containing computer-controlled machine tools loaded and unloaded by robots. Fanuc has estimated that ten times the capital investment would have been required for a conventional plant with the same capacity. The labor force of 100 would also have been 10 times larger for a conventional machining capability. This was not an investment proposed by a foreman or industrial engineer

seeking to shave direct labor costs and improve productivity. It demanded a vision of what could be accomplished by a dramatic change. It demanded a broad analysis of the company's competitive position and long-term strategy. It demanded an imaginative approach to implementation, and a top-management commitment of the resources necessary to make things happen. Given the same vision and sound strategic planning, I am confident most top managements would conclude that an investment of this type would be attractive enough to exceed their financial hurdle rates.

Here is another example. Yamazaki Machinery Works, Ltd., makes parts for computer-controlled lathes and machining centers in a new $20-million plant near Nagoya. In the daytime, 12 workers man the plant; at night, only a lone watchman is on duty while the machines keep working. A conventional plant with similar capacity would require about 215 employees, and nearly four times as many machines. Again, I am sure that a financial evaluation of this investment would appear quite attractive to any of our own companies, even with the most pessimistic of assumptions.

There are many more examples like these from Japanese industry. Unfortunately, nothing even remotely comparable is now happening here in our country, or, for that matter, anywhere else except in Japan. This disturbing situation lends emphasis to the critical need to meet the new industrial competition.

Assuming that many U.S. companies will eventually commit themselves to a major, technological upgrading of their manufacturing facilities, what are apt to be the limiting factors? Will they be financial? I think not. Experience suggests that the rate of progress will be driven more by availability of the skilled people necessary to plan and implement the change. This does not imply that a massive program of the type envisioned would not place a severe, near-term financial strain on most of our companies. However, it does imply that the required application of new investment would, of necessity, be stretched out over a long enough period to make it affordable.

Two Critical Questions

We face a management challenge that appears to pose two critical questions. First, will individual business strategies be developed in a manner that points out the necessity for investing in factories of the future? Second, will our top managements be convinced of the necessity, and of the financial viability, for making the required large investments?

Survival in many of U.S. businesses would appear to depend on an emphatic "yes" answer to both of these questions. Concerning the investment question, we need some changes in the way we look at the financial return for investments of this type. More effort is required to ensure that the evaluation approach and underlying assumptions are realistic. It is worth saying again: We need to consider more adequately the long-term competitive environment, and to factor in the negative impact of not making the investment. This problem appears to be solvable, and seems to be getting more and more management attention in many of U.S. companies. I hope that our future actions prove to the world that U.S. industry was able to meet the challenge.

Market Competition and Manufacturing Strategies
Thomas L. Skelly

In the past four or five years, it has become increasingly clear that worldwide market competition in the electronics industry places a heavy emphasis on product quality, reliability and responsiveness to a wide variety of customer-satisfaction measurements. In order to compete in the 1980's and 1990's, a better understanding of manufacturing strategies that influence product cost, asset management, and delivery systems is required at the corporate level. Implementation planning must be on a long-range basis and cannot be tied to short-term financial planning. The implementation strategies must be flexible so they can handle a variety of product changes and variations, without significant impact on floor layouts and personnel training. In the areas of manufacturing computer systems, automation of material flow, and the use of robotics in assembling products, we are moving out of the evolutionary phase of manufacturing into a revolutionary phase. In the past ten to fifteen years, a significant amount of offshore manufacturing has taken place because of available cheap labor in those marketplaces. With, however, the implementation of the new manufacturing strategies and a continuing reduced direct-labor content in new products, the advantages for offshore manufacture will decrease, and the disadvantages of material asset control, design change implementation, and the shortening of product life cycles will become the dominant factors in selecting manufacturing locations.

The Challenge Industry Must Meet
Thomas J. Murrin

We must recognize the crucial importance of quality in the fight for market share. The Japanese have undoubtedly been the classic example in demonstrating that quality and reliability will capture markets—as seen by their success with motorcycles, automobiles, machine tools, and home electronics, to name a few.

U.S. industry must realize that conventional wisdom in regard to the presumed high cost of quality is no longer valid. Doing it right the first time does not cost more money; rather, it saves money. This is clearly one of the main reasons why the Japanese have become so productive in all the industrial segments in which they have concentrated.

Conversely, one of the key reasons for productivity problems in the United States is the quality of our industrial output. Producing more—inefficiently and at the expense of quality—is no way to increase productivity. Putting more inspectors on the line to find the mistakes is the wrong approach. Doing something over, because it was not done right the first time, decreases efficiency, wastes money, and lowers productivity. A typical U.S. factory routinely has "unquality" costs averaging 15 to 30 percent of annual sales billed. It is quite easy, with the new advances in technology, to cut that figure at least in half. That saving can be as big as the company's profit margin; in other words, profitability can be doubled. Quality and productivity go hand in hand. Simply stated, improved productivity and improved profitability are inevitable by-products of improved quality.

We must make quality a way of life in all that we do. We cannot merely dictate that our products and services be of the highest quality—rather, we have to build quality into each and every phase of corporate life. We need to make continuous total quality improvement the guide for research and development, for product designs, for product manufacturing, and for product support. We need to think continuous total quality improvement in our human-resource programs: hiring, career development and training, and labor relations. Quality must become an attitude that permeates the entire operation.

The Information Continuum:
A Redistribution of Service and
Intelligence Functions
Vincent E. Giuliano

What is the difference in information handling that distinguishes organizations that are highly competitive, highly successful, highly evolving, from organizations that seem to be stolid and noncompetitive? What is needed for the second kind of organization to convert to the first kind—one with vitality, with the capacity to grow?

The difference is not whether an organization handles or processes information. The open secret is that every organization is in the business of handling information. Communicating, coordinating inputs, coordinating employees and machines, coordinating suppliers and customers and third parties—that is the business of any organization. Nor is the difference one of high technology.

The difference is found in what information is gathered; what information is listened to; and how information is handled. The difference can be most easily explained in terms of the informational context—that is, the set of implicit assumptions, the operational culture, that dictate the information habits of the organization and set the limits within which the organization functions.

The Preindustrial Shop

The information continuum can be divided into three stages: preindustrial, industrial and informational.

I would like to start with the preindustrial stage because I was exposed to it in my childhood—in my Uncle Gigi's tailoring business, which was a uniform-manufacturing shop. He made uniforms for firemen, policemen and band members. There was an open manufacturing area, with cutting tables and sewing tables. The business was run almost entirely by Italian immigrants. Gigi, the boss, had a big office with sliding windows in the middle. His office was surrounded by the offices of three sons and one son-in-law.

Gigi's policy for the business was to go out and get business—wherever the business was. As an example, one day Laurice, the manager of marketing, was at the local high school talking with the teacher in charge of the band. The big game was coming up, and Laurice phoned Uncle Gigi to ask if they could close on a sale for 85 band uniforms. Gigi quickly called the others together and asked them whether they could handle making 85 number-62 uniforms with number-13 blue-serge cloth and big black leather belts. Hector, who was in charge of the shop, called the shop supervisor on the floor to discuss which people could handle the order. At the same time, Eros, in charge of purchasing, called United Cloth, with which he had a good relationship, to find out if the right kind of cloth was available. Meanwhile, Gigi asked Norris to find out when delivery had to be made and what an acceptable price would be. (It turned out to be $65, because a competitor had bid $68.) Gigi then talked to Hector about scheduling the job, and possibly moving an operator from the buttonhole machine to the cutting machine.

In the course of a 15-minute, dynamic process (what would today be called a real-time decision system), a good deal of information input was correlated in real time. Knowledge about the industry and about production processing were brought to bear on the discussion. Gigi phoned Laurice, his marketing man, at the school to accept the deal, and also to offer seven spangled batons and helmets for the cheerleaders, "just to close the sale."

Although Gigi's shop did not always work that effectively, it might be useful to look at some of the success factors. The first was the ability to correlate information rapidly. The second was the ability to utilize human resources and knowledge in the context of trust and open, informal communication. Of course, it was a family business and all the key executives had close ties to one another. There were absolutely minimal paperwork requirements: There were no bureaucratic boundaries to cross. The verbal commitments between Eros and United Cloth, between Laurice at the high school and Gigi in the office, were as good as a written contract. One's word was one's bond in the garment industry. A third success factor was, in sophisticated terms, "flexible information feedback for dynamic reallocation of human and machine resources in all stages of the production planning, marketing and production processes."

What are the significant characteristics of a preindustrial organization like this one? It is unorganized, unplanned, participative and flexible. Worker experience is a vital contribution to the success of the enterprise. Even today there are garment-district shops run essentially like this. It is still a very suitable form of organization for a small business.

The Industrial-Age Organization

The success factors of the classical manufacturing enterprise are well-known. Among them are standardization, mass markets, economy of scale in all aspects (e.g., national advertising permits large production runs), efficiency, centralization, routine operations. But the close working relationships among individuals have been replaced by very complex organizations and bureaucratic boundaries. As a result, the ability to function in real time is lost. Instead the enterprises function in bureaucratic time; information moves as the paper that contains the information moves. And if we look at the content of information flows in this classical manufacturing enterprise, we find a shift in emphasis from highly dynamic intermixing of policy and operational information to the routine flow of operational information—daily, weekly and monthly reports, accounting, orders, production schedules, material flow, and the like.

The information systems, although relatively simple, are not well linked. And familiarity with and responsibility for the information systems pass from the key executives to an information priesthood. Generally, these systems were well-suited to batch mainframe computing. They were created as an analogue of the production system, using an industrial engineering model.

Another drawback of the classical manufacturing enterprise is inflexibility. It is marked, as Goldhar puts it, by "long runs of standard products...in which change is barred at the door." Such an enterprise typically has reactive management, a want of concern for people, low morale, and unionism. The worker is regarded as an extension of the machine, as its arm or leg or foot or finger. There is a narrow definition of productivity. The focus is on input measures instead of output measures. Is the worker present? Does the worker look awake? Does the worker seem to be working? All in all, the utilization of human resources is rather low.

Now there is an analogue to information processing that can be found in organisms. Even the lowest form of animals have what is called unconscious or automatic information processing. Breathing, digesting and heart beat are all short-term information loops. They correspond in the corporation to the payroll, the customer billing, inventory renewal, and routine operational data handling.

Higher animals—such as dogs and cats—have a higher level of information processing. They can walk, eat and drink, activities that require some thought and perhaps short-term planning. This thought and planning corresponds to the functions of information processing associated with accounting, plant maintenance, operating a production line, setting inventory stock levels, or routine administrative work.

I submit that most industrial-era organizations have not progressed beyond these two levels of information processing that higher animals perform. These organizations have not moved to the human level of thoughtfulness or planning.

The Information-Era Organization

In the information-era organization, we find different success factors: participative management, focus on quality, demassification, targeted markets, more product variety, short product-life cycles. The management is smart and responsive. It is strategy and planning oriented. It gives adequate emphasis to the long term, while not disregarding the short term. It is knowledge and information-driven, and the manufacturing function is an integral aspect of operations. As for the major information relationships among different components involved in manufacturing, users, customers and suppliers, everything is closely connected to everything else. That is one major lesson.

Another is the emphasis on strategic planning and guidance information, and the linkage of functional subsystems. The system is held together by use of data bases and electronic communications that link the operational components—human and machines. The information system creation becomes a responsibility of all management. What this model represents is a return to the preindustrial shop, admittedly on a much larger and more complex scale. The role of information technology is to make possible a recreation of Uncle Gigi's smoothly working, person-centered organization. It permits the organization to shift from preoccupation with minimum cost to maximum effectiveness and to economy of scope. This third level of information processing can be called very highly conscious information processing. Finally, the information-era organization is strategy, knowledge, and market-driven rather than tradition-driven.

Moving to the Information-Era Organization

How does a firm move to this form of organization from the classical manufacturing enterprise, how does it shift from what we are to what we are determined to be? First, management must realize that the firm has options in defining its business in terms of what it does. It is a point any management striving for an information-era organization must keep in mind.

Another success factor in this transition is that the responsibility for the management of information can no longer be vested solely in the information priesthood, or the key people who are in charge of information. Of course, there has to be a body of expertise, but the responsibility for the management of information is essentially the responsibility for the identification of user needs, the responsibility for taking the initiative to create an appropriate system. These have to be distributed throughout the organization, from the bottom up and the top down. That means that the chief information manager in the company has to be the CEO. That is not a contradiction in terms because the organization is primarily concerned with information communication, and the CEO is in charge of the organization.

The information-era organization has a context of participative management, desynchronization of the machine as the extension of the worker, concern for quality, concern with mobilizing and developing the human capacity. I agree with those who assert that if we are capable of creating these contexts in our organizations, we shall have no problem in doing well as a nation.

Making Technological Changes
James E. Ashton

When one talks about change to U.S. managers, especially manufacturing-oriented managers, one tends to hear about its disruptive aspects. In fact it is not uncommon for a manufacturing manager to say if "they" would just cut out all the changes, "we" could produce the product efficiently.

Most companies have a management style that is quite conducive to producing a high volume of products efficiently in a steady state condition. It is not at all conducive to making changes. We tend, therefore, to resist making changes. And when we do make changes, they always take longer than we said they would, and cost more than we said they would, and sometimes they do not work as well as we said they would. So long as there is that attitude toward change, and so long as we manage in the way we have, we are going to have trouble adopting new technologies, as well as in making other changes that are at least as important in terms of improving productivity.

We hear lots of references to management, to the style and the kind of management culture we ought to have. We hear people say that we have to "manage" the work force better so we can put these new automated factories on stream and persuade the workers to accept them. Some say that the problem is not with production workers, it is in the wasteland of middle management where change is resisted. It is also very common to hear that the first-line supervisor is the key. The implication of all these statements is that if we are successfully to introduce change, we have to educate production workers, supervisors and middle management so they do not resist it. One of the recipes is for top executives to be clearly in front, to demonstrate commitment, so everybody will adapt to and adopt change.

It has to start at the top. But it is not enough for senior management to say that productivity is important or automation is important, or funding will be ample. Top management has to do this, but it also has to have a style that will eventually pervade an organization, that will set the tone for it.

It is fairly ridiculous to talk about installing participative or flexible or innovative people-oriented management in the organization, about middle management and first-line supervisors who believe in team building and who take reasonable technological risks, if the people at the top are autocratic or inflexible or totally numbers-oriented, or risk-adverse, or unforgiving. It is not what you say; it is what you do. In the end, top management needs to demonstrate its willingness to employ a suitable style if a company is adroitly to capitalize on the new opportunities in manufacturing.

At General Dynamics, I was involved in a changeover in a Fort Worth plant. There were approximately 8,000 people in the production department. I thought that because of inertia, the unwillingness of workers to change the way they did things, we probably could not change the basic style, the culture, the way things were done, in less than ten years. After a couple of years, however, we had altered procedures not just at my head-of-operations level, but also at the first-line supervisory and the middle-management levels. As a result, we had a good record of success with the introduction of new technologies and other sorts of automation.

These were alterations driven from the top by a change in style and a change in attitude, a determination that we were going to do things differently and better, and that after we changed some things, we would change others for the better, and after that, still more changes would ensue. This would be an endless journey toward improvement, not a journey with a destination.

After a couple of years workers well below the top management level had accepted this message and some of them were even preaching it. None of this would have happened, nor would success stories have been told about that plant, without management's change in attitude.

Making the Factory of the Future a Reality
Stephen R. Rosenthal

What has to be done to make the concept of the factory of the future into a reality? And how do we begin to do it?

I have spent a year doing research on factory automation in the United States and I have talked with a large number of users, suppliers and other experts. Some specific findings of my research are:

• Leading-edge users learn by doing. There is no magic in the steps executives in automated companies have taken. They have developed a sense of direction for automation, they have had supportive management along the way, and they have gradually built a base of experience that allows them to progress to more difficult types of innovations.
• Many observers believe that most manufacturers are not sophisticated customers for factory-automation technology. They possess a limited understanding of what the technologies are, of how they work, and, even more disturbing, of their own needs.
• Inadequate attention is being paid to the long-term strategic benefits of factory automation. One wonders why.
• Most manufacturers will not reduce their risks by waiting until technology gets better. Broad technology exists; what is needed is experience with using it.

Factory Economics and Business Strategy
Robert J. Mayer

Future factories will lower manufacturing cost, increase the importance of scale relative to focus, change the optimal plant size, and decrease the importance of accumulated volume on cost. These changes in factory economics will have major implications for business strategy.

Strategic Implications

Factory flexibility will broaden the span of products any company can manufacture economically. Product segments will be defined by the basic manufacturing process—for example, milled metal parts, molded plastics, and fabricated metals; and specialized designs will be produced with the economics of high-volume production of commodity products. Finally, new competitors will enter traditional markets.

More important, the new factory economics will significantly affect the value-added structure and change the basis of competition. For example, manufacturing is now a primary basis of competition for discrete products, with manufacturing costs totaling 50 to 60 percent of total costs. Since, with factory-of-the-future economics, manufacturing cost will decrease significantly, marketing and selling will become the primary bases of competition. As a result, the focus of segmentation will shift from products to markets.

Product segments will expand from their present narrowly defined scope. In the future, segments will be defined more by the manufacturing process than by product end-use. For example, manufacturing competitive advantage will reflect how well a company *manufactures* milled metal products, instead of the end products themselves.

Markets will be more narrowly defined as companies organize to serve specific customer needs such as *service level* (lead time, quality, technical support), *customer size and fragmentation* (distribution channels), and *engineered* versus *mass-produced* products. In the future, these market segments will be based on focused markets, customer access, and service level. Competitive advantage will be built upon the total production volume of scale across a wide range of products at low cost to serve more narrowly defined market segments.

If the economics of the factory of the future are so compelling, why is factory automation not moving at a faster pace? Some technology gaps impede progress, such as the lack of factory-wide data bases, consistent standards among equipment manufacturers, and well-functioning robots. Some human factors present significant hurdles: attitudinal resistance by both white- and blue-collar workers, the need to retrain blue-collar employees, the need to make changes in organization structure and accountability patterns. Finally, costs sunk in present equipment and systems make managements reluctant to change.

Strategic Requirements

It is competition that makes investment in the factory of the future a strategic issue. The winning strategic manufacturing response requires understanding of market opportunities and requirements for manufacturing; knowing the competition because it is going to change; and establishing the appropriate plant focus and deployment strategy advantage required to succeed in the newly defined markets.

The first step in setting the strategy requires segmenting manufacturing into strategic manufacturing units (SMU's) that have common marketing, product and manufacturing characteristics. The major market characteristics include size, volume, growth rate, demand variability, demographics, response time, and customer order size. The key product characteristics are size, shape, complexity, position in the life cycle, the number of product variations, degree of customization, and the precision of product. For manufacturing, the important characteristics are process complexity, process lead time, and ease of alternative sourcing. It is possible to assign all products, no matter what their functional use, to SMU's. The SMU's will be focused on key success requirements dictated by the marketplace, as the diagram illustrates.

Total factory focus (technology and organizational

| SMU I | • Standard Product
• Stable Product Design
• Low Demand Variability
• High Response Time |

KEY SUCCESS REQUIREMENTS

PRICE

| SMU II | • Product Variation
• High Demand Variability
• Moderate/Low Volume
• Intermediate Response Time |

FLEXIBILITY

| SMU III | • Engineered Specific Product
• High Demand Variability
• Long Lead Times |

PRODUCT INNOVATION

structure) and the deployment strategy for the production base can then be established through analysis of the key factors that influence scale and logistics economics. Trade-off analyses of the major factors that affect aggregate factory scale, such as shared technologies and service functions, for the anticipated market volume will establish the appropriate factory configuration and size. Economics of the manufacturing location relative to sourcing and market will establish the deployment strategy. With a comprehensive manufacturing strategy in place, management will be in an excellent position to establish an investment plan to provide for the development and application of these future technologies in an orderly way to achieve a dominant competitive position.

The factory of the future will potentially give all producers the same product cost across broad product categories. Those who do not invest in advanced manufacturing technology will probably be out of the game in the future; the winners will be those who focus their manufacturing and competitive strategy on the key success factors in narrowly defined market segments.

Part IV
Putting the New Technology in Place

Technological Advances that Alter Competition
Jack Wickham

Someone once said that all the natural resources on earth are essentially free and the only reason it costs money to buy a barrel of oil or an ounce of gold is because of all the bother and expense of locating these things, extracting them from the earth, transporting them, purifying them, refining them, forming and packaging them, and distributing them. The same thing is true with technology. For most industries, all the technology that is required to make an individual company strongly competitive is already well developed and readily available. The problem is in locating the most suitable technology and, once it is located, adapting it to the need at hand. If all businesses were the same, most companies could play "follow the leader," with each business copying the strategies and tactics of the leaders in its field.

But, of course, things do not work that way. Any business that has tried to imitate exactly another business has found itself in trouble sooner or later. It turns out that no two businesses are ever truly identical. Each business' markets are unique; so are its products, its manufacturing, its work force, and its management culture. The challenge then, is to identify the most appropriate technology for a particular business and utilize it effectively.

There is much feeling today that the selection and utilization of technology are not being done very well in the United States. All over this country companies are struggling with this problem.

In a recent article, John Baxter discussed the productivity of capital stock—machinery and equipment—used in manufacturing. He claimed that the negative impact of poor equipment productivity on industry and the U.S. economy is just as great as poor labor productivity. I would say it is greater. The effect of poor equipment selection and spending is an even more serious problem in the United States than is poor labor productivity.

Some of the figures he cited are arresting. Using real 1972 dollars of output per real dollar of investment in net depreciated equipment, he found the figure for 1973 was $2.55; by 1976, the figure had declined to $2.10; by 1980, to $1.76; and by 1982, to $1.47. One might argue with his numbers or his relative values, but I do not think there is any question that the trend he described reflects reality.[1]

He attributed this decline to the lagging economy, which has been forcing plants to operate below optimum levels. But plants have been doing that for ten years, and one would think that in ten years everyone would get acclimated to whatever operating level was required. The inescapable fact is that, for whatever reason, the productivity of capital invested has been continuously declining for ten years.

Not every industry has this problem, of course. Some U.S. companies and industries seem to be able to absorb and utilize technology very effectively—for instance, the semiconductor business. Because of its high growth rate, perhaps that business has found it easier to maintain a good level of efficiency.

Likewise, some countries seem to have fared better than the United States. Japan comes to mind at once. But the Japanese themselves deprecate the idea that their technology is any better than anyone else's. They only claim that they use technology better. In conversations I have had with people from the Japanese machine tool industry, they invariably express wonder at the equipment selections that many Americans make. They will say that Americans always want to go first class, that Americans will spend far more than the Japanese to

[1]John Baxter, "Plant, Equipment, Productivity Down." *Iron Age.* January 21, 1983, pp. 41-43.

perform the same function. In my experience, they are too often right. Overspending for equipment is symptomatic of an inability to use technology effectively.

This inability quickly translates into an inability to use money effectively. It is common to find U.S. companies that are spending too much on machines and equipment. Ironically, often these same companies have spent too little for years, only to be suddenly converted to spending too much on marginally productive improvements.

In the manufacturing technology area, the tendency to overspend to poor effect is particularly apparent. The manufacturing technology scene currently is dominated by such concepts as CNC, high-speed machining, and just-in-time processing. These are all valid concepts, and, if intelligently incorporated into the business, they will enhance the manufacturing capability of any company. But what we often see is an all-too-familiar dichotomy. The manufacturer either largely ignores the concepts, or abandons all caution and pursues one or another single-mindedly. Either extreme is undesirable.

Three Examples

Several years ago, my associates and I built a high-speed machining machine for a company that produced small die-cast machine parts. The machine in question was tooled for several parts, one of which ran to a volume of about 100,000 units a year. On previous equipment, it had taken a little over one minute to process this particular part. With the new equipment, the floor-to-floor cycle was eight seconds, about one-ninth of the previous time. So in supplying the equipment, we established a standard cycle or costing time of twelve seconds; we took the floor-to-floor time of eight seconds and added a very generous 50 percent allowance.

After the manufacturing plant took delivery on the equipment, the manufacturing engineer told us that he had negotiated with shop people and established a standard of 17 seconds on the equipment, as against the 12 seconds that had been recommended. This had been done without even running the machine. A week later, the machine was in production and the plant discovered that it could not even make a 22-second rate. I thought I should have a look, because I had run the equipment myself and knew it was capable of an eight-second cycle. At the plant, I discovered that the part was being manually handled five times! An employee was picking each part out of the in-basket and putting it on the edge of the machine, picking it up from there and putting it into the machine, removing it from the machine and replacing it on the machine's edge, then putting it on a table where he would blow the chips off. Finally he would gauge the part and put it in a basket.

Of those extra handlings, only two were justified: one from the in-basket into the machine, and the other out of

the machine and into the basket that took finished parts. The additional three handlings took ten seconds. That particular plant had always handled parts that way. With the old cycle, the three extra handlings had increased costs by about 15 percent. With the new cycle, the three additional handlings cost 83 percent extra.

One might think that once the problem was pinpointed, this story would have a happy ending. But in fact the plant never really did improve its material handling, even after the manufacturing engineer understood the problem. He was happy with 22 seconds because this was one-third of the previous cycle. His management regarded the whole issue as not worthy of its concern, and so an improvement that was available at no additional cost was forfeited. As a result, the plant was soon out of capacity and needed another machine, one that might never have been required had better methods engineering been employed.

The moral of this story is that the technology was made available and even delivered to the plant, but the company's managers were unable to utilize it fully because they did not understand how to integrate it into their business. The net result was excessive investment in equipment. For its efforts in this program, the company had improved its competitiveness only marginally. I submit that marginal improvements are not what most U.S. companies need today.

A second example involves a company that produced a variety of parts in somewhat smaller volumes than the first firm. Recall that the first company had an annual production volume of 100,000 of one part. For the second company, the annual volume was 60,000 units. Its plant had been plagued with setup and changeover problems for years. Management finally decided to buy a modern, high-speed flexible machine, but it put only two parts on the machine, perceiving that that was enough to yield a return on its investment. The equipment was greatly under-utilized. The company believed that labor costs for one or two of the highest volume parts were the only really important costs. It failed to capitalize fully on the capability of the machine. It could easily have had a "free ride" on that equipment for some lower volume parts.

A final example: The management of still another company had decided to convert to just-in-time manufacturing, Japanese style. Previously its plants had been organized around processers. There was a department of screw machines, a department of grinders, and so forth. Most of the equipment was old and well along in its depreciation schedule; but for its age, it was quite productive—that is, it produced parts at a rapid rate. However, it took many hours to change these machines over, which did not fit the just-in-time concept at all. So the decision was made to abandon the old equipment and obtain new equipment that would change over rapidly. But the new equipment did not produce as fast as the old equipment, necessitating more new machines than old ones. The whole program bogged down rapidly when management began to see that the financial return was becoming negative. The net result was that a program embarked on to increase the efficiency of the operation produced no positive gain and incurred a substantial amount of new debt. The company's ill-advised foray into just-in-time manufacturing turned out to be an economic failure.

These stories are not exaggerations. This kind of thing is happening all over the country. I submit that because most U.S. companies are not technology driven, they have managers who do not relate to the technological side of the business. This is particularly true of older companies serving mature markets.

What Can Be Done?

Is the solution to replace a company's top managers with people of technical backgrounds? In our experience that would not do much good.

The real problem is that most business managers, regardless of background, do not have enough feel for the basics of the business; and this is particularly true in product engineering and in manufacturing. As one consultant has put it, most U.S. managers do not know enough about how their businesses actually work. It cannot do much good to employ new strategies or to reorganize if one does not know in what direction to move. And one cannot know that without knowing what is wrong, or in what direction opportunities lie.

In the first company I described, the manufacturing people failed to establish good engineering methods, with the result that they ensured poor productivity. At the second company, management failed to appreciate how poorly it was utilizing its new equipment. And the third company pursued just-in-time philosophy to the point of negative return because management was ignorant of more appropriate alternatives.

In all three companies any new strategies and reorganizations would not do much good. Managing the technical side of many U.S. companies is now a little like managing a locomotive from the last car in a passenger train. Someone so located might notice that the rate at which the telegraph poles are passing is slowing. Yet we should expect to be misled if the only sense we had of the locomotive was passing telephone poles. The speed of the poles is evidence of the pace of progress, but it gives no real clue as to how to optimize or to improve the pace. But this is exactly what many U.S. managers are doing: They count money, or, more accurately, the speed with which it is accumulated. When money is being accumulated rapidly—when profits are high—management resolves to continue doing whatever it is now doing because that seems to be working. As circumstances

change, for whatever reasons, a change in course is then deemed necessary.

This is what I call reactive management. What we need in U.S. companies today is anticipative management: Management has to foresee the problems that are coming because it understands the business and its direction well enough to do so.

Fortunately, this can be done without transforming every manager into a thoroughly technical type. To manage anticipatively the progress of a locomotive, it is not necessary to know how to design a locomotive. It is, however, necessary to have a fundamental understanding of how one works and, beyond that, to understand how to optimize its performance, what its capability limits are, and what tests to employ to determine how nearly those limits are being approached.

In a manufacturing company, people at all levels have to develop a sufficient technical understanding and absorb a certain amount of technical training. Developing the work force, expanding an organization's technical capability, selecting the right machines and equipment—all these things require enlightened, knowledgeable management. One cannot sit at the rear of the train and have any hope of optimizing a locomotive's performance.

Computer-Integrated Manufacturing
M. Eugene Merchant

One of my major responsibilities is to observe and evalute research, development and implementation of new manufacturing technology throughout the world. Until recent years, I found progress to be slow and highly incremental. However, the emergence of the digital computer as a working tool in industry has changed that. A wholly new approach to manufacturing has evolved, namely the generic concept of *computer-integrated manufacturing,* and it is now being researched, developed and implemented in many countries. This approach has the ability to integrate all of the various elements of the total system of manufacturing, starting with the design of the product and going through the entire production process to the final shipment of finished products—fully assembled, inspected and ready for use. CIM also has the capability to optimize and to automate both the operations within these elements *and* the total system—and to do that on-line and flexibly.

In spite of the fact that implementation of CIM is still in its infancy, it has already demonstrated far greater potential to increase manufacturing productivity and quality and to reduce manufacturing costs (i.e., create real, tangible wealth more cost effectively) than any other technology that has appeared on the scene since the onset of the Industrial Revolution. Thus it is being recognized everywhere as the beginning of the second industrial revolution.

An indication of this potential can be gleaned from performance experience already obtained with computer-integrated systems of machine tools and related production equipment. These systems, commonly known as flexible manufacturing systems (FMS), are to some extent microcosms of the future total system of computer-integrated manufacturing. The most advanced such systems (even though equivalent systems are available from U.S. producers) have been first put in place abroad. Here are some examples.

Messerschmitt's Augsburg Plant

The first such system is that installed at Messerschmitt-Bolkow-Blohm in Augsburg, West Germany, producing titanium parts for the Tornado fighter plane. There are some 28 numerically controlled (NC) machine tools operating under coordinated computer control within the system. Supporting these are two other main subsystems. The first is an automated workpiece transfer system bringing workpieces to and from the machine tools by means of computer-controlled carts. The second is a fully automated tool-transport and tool-changing system. This brings tools to each machine via an overhead network. It then automatically transfers the tools to a continuous elevator tool storage, which in turn interfaces with the automatic tool-changing mechanism of the machine tool. All three of these subsystems—the machine tools, the work-transfer system, and the tool-transfer system—are coordinated, controlled and automated by a hierarchical distributed computer system.

Now for the results—the illustration of the potential power of this technology. The machines in the system are cutting metal 75 to 80 percent of the time, instead of the usual 15 to 30 percent obtained with machines that are not part of such a system. The lead time for the Tornado is 18 months, compared to 30 months for an equivalent plane produced conventionally. When compared with producing the same parts with identical numerically controlled machine tools not part of such a system, the system has reduced the required number of skilled machinists by 44 percent, the required floor space by 39 percent, the part-flow time in the factory by 25 percent, and the required capital investment by 9 percent.

In addition, nonquantified benefits have been experienced. Quality has been increased, manifesting itself in the form of higher reproducibility of the dimensions of the machined parts, lower rework costs, and lower scrap rates. This, in turn, has resulted in lower quality-assurance costs. Also, adherence to production schedules is much improved and the usual flood of paper has been considerably decreased. And working conditions are improved because of the decreased risk of accidents and the relief from heavy physical labor and monotonous work. Here is technology of tremendous potential power.

Japanese Examples

The second example is an essentially *unmanned* FMS installed at Niigata Engineering Company's internal combustion engine plant in Niigata, Japan, at a cost of about $2.5 million. It is machining 30 different types of diesel engine cylinder heads in lot sizes ranging from six to thirty parts. A robot mounts the simpler parts on pallets automatically. The system produces parts, 24 hours per day, and runs completely unattended at night.

Now for the savings: Only six machines are required to produce the parts, compared with thirty-one (including six NC) required conventionally (an 81 percent reduction); the number of operators has been reduced from thirty-one to four (an 87 percent reduction); and the lead time for these parts has been reduced from sixteen days to four.

The third example also comes from Japan. It is a factory that Fanuc Ltd. has recently put into operation for producing robots and small machine tools, the machining section of which operates almost wholly unattended on the night shift. There are 29 machining cells in this section (22 machining centers served by automatic pallet changers and seven robot-served cells), each consisting of one or more NC machine tools and a robot or pallet changer to keep the machine or machines loaded with parts during the night. Workpieces, on pallets, are transported to and from the cells and computer-controlled automatic stacker cranes by computer-controlled wire-guided carts.

The results? During the day there are a total of 19 workers on the machining floor. On the night shift there is no one on the machining floor, and only one man in the control room, with the machines producing parts unattended during the night. During the 24-hour period, machine availability runs close to 100 percent, and machine utilization averages 65 to 70 percent. As a result, this 220,000 square-foot factory is producing 100 robots, 75 machining centers, and 75 EDM (electro-discharge-machinery) wire-cut machines per month. What happens if something goes wrong at night? There are monitoring systems on many of the machines. (The other machines do not need such systems because of their dependability.) The system monitors such operating characteristics as spindle motor current, elapsed cutting time per tool, and the integrity of drills. They shut the machine down at night if anything goes wrong, and provide a diagnosis of the failure so that the workers will know what corrective action to take in the morning.

Quite a number of other Japanese companies are in various stages of implementation of computer-controlled, unattended night-shift operations. Having that capability, many of these companies are now beginning to take advantage of not only 24-hour operation, but also the great versatility of these computer-controlled machines and systems to accomplish just-in-time production. They let the requirements of the assembly floor of the manufacturing facility "pull" the needed parts through the factory, rather than depending on scheduling to "push" them through. They accomplish this by loading these highly flexible cells and systems in one 24-hour period with just the mix of parts that will be needed on the assembly floor in the next 24-hour period. Thus, work in progress is reduced virtually to zero, freeing up tremendous amounts of idle capital.

As I mentioned earlier, computer integrated manufacturing is currently being put to work more rapidly and effectively in the manufacturing industry of other countries than in that of the United States.

The Moral of the Story

It is ironic that although the lion's share of basic CIM knowledge and technology that is gradually being put to work has been developed in this country, U.S. industry has not moved as fast as industry in some other countries to exploit this knowledge and technology. There are those who say that there is no future in manufacturing for U.S. industry—that instead the future is in high technology. Most regrettably, this view is completely blind to the reality that, at present, *manufacturing is high technology!* For any manufacturing company that is not hi-tech, or on the way to becoming hi-tech, there is likely to be *no* future!

Management Problems of Technological Change
Leo H. Everitt

Steering a company through technological changeover may be the hardest part of managing change. Technology frightens most company managements. Even when it is working right, it tends to be mysterious. When something goes awry, some systems take on lives of their own with consequences for next quarter's profits.

No wonder that many industries stick with the doctrine: If it isn't broke, don't fix it. Manage for stability; treat the factory as a cash cow. There is no need to understand technology as long as the existing factory can be milked. The trouble was, and is, that technology has not been standing still. Those who know how to exploit its advances have effected changes in both products and the processes that produce them. But even when these opportunities are seized at the technical level, the strategic implications for the enterprise are not always perceived at the top corporate level. In too many companies, management continues to steer the boat by looking back to be sure that the wake stays straight.

Putting New Technology in Existing Plants
James A. Baker

In our rush to meet world industrial competition, we seem to be focusing on trying to construct high-tech "Silicon Valleys" all over the United States, and on enlarging service businesses. General Electric's attitude is that if America abandons its manufacturing base in favor of services, it faces real disaster. The technology for automating engineering and manufacturing operations—the key to reviving industrial America—is available. All that is needed is a strong management commitment and the courage to try it.

The Technical Systems Sector of GE has invested more than $500 million over the past two years in new products, acquisitions and technology that can turn things around for U.S. manufacturing and can establish for our company a leadership role in a market that may well reach $30 billion by the end of this decade. GE operates 377 factories, and despite our growth in the services sector (in finance and the like), we are still overwhelmingly a manufacturing company—the largest diverse manufacturing company in the world. GE is not ashamed of its smokestacks, and it is not afraid of the Japanese. After competing with them all over the world, however, I hasten to add that they have our respect.

Three examples from GE spell out *my* idea of how to meet the new industrial competition.

The General Electric Company is in the process of making the largest single factory-automation investment in its history. And it is not in robots, or integrated circuits, or CT scanners, or jet engines. It is in a 70-year-old factory in Erie, Pennsylvania, the headquarters of a GE business Thomas Edison started: locomotives. A few years ago, the same writing that appeared on the factory walls in Allentown and Detroit began to appear at Erie: aging manufacturing equipment, a slow market, increasing foreign competition, layoffs, and so on. We decided that we *liked* building locomotives, that GE had the technology to build the world's best, at the best price, and that no one—the Japanese, the French, or anyone else—was going to run us out of business, or out of town. In early 1983, the first stage of an electronic heart transplant for that old factory was completed. Motor frames that used to require *16* days and *64* skilled machinists to complete, now take *16* hours and *2* workers.

When the automation of this factory is completed, we will be able to produce one-third more locomotives in virtually the same floor area, and we will be employing 10 percent *more* people. Everyone wins, except possibly our competitors. Incidentally, we recently won an order for over 60 lomocotives. One reason the customer gave for selecting GE was that the automation in our plant would result in better product quality and reliability.

A textile factory was built in 1922 in Somersworth, New Hampshire. GE bought it in 1947 and began to make electric meters there. A few years ago, we had to decide whether to move to a new location where we would have more space, or to find a way to make more meters more efficiently within those same old walls. We chose the latter course, installing some advanced material-handling and warehousing equipment, adding numerically controlled machine tools, bringing computers in by the truckload, and marching in the robots.

As a result, shop costs are lower due to a 30 percent reduction in material-handling costs. Some 10,000 square feet of floor space was freed. The machine-monitoring system, working with numerically controlled machine tools, has increased productivity by 15 percent, while machine downtime has been cut in half. Use of the assembly robot doubled parts production and greatly improved quality.

In Louisville, Kentucky, a 30-year-old factory makes GE ranges, refrigerators and dishwashers. This is a classic U.S. business: Hit hard by the recession, competition from Japan and Korea, aging equipment, labor problems, high costs and layoffs, there were doubts about whether GE, the biggest employer in the city, would stay.

We announced to the community that we were going to make an investment to automate the Louisville plant. Our objective was not to displace people, but to find a way to improve product quality and features. In the Spring of 1983, after investing $38 million, GE dedicated Project "C." This is not a space program or a secret laser project, but just a way to make a top-quality dishwasher at a competitive price, and to keep an old business in the town it grew up in.

On the day that Project "C" was dedicated, the politicians came, the Governor sent a telegram, and virtually every one of the 900 workers in that building voluntarily wore T-shirts that said "GE Is Me." The prevailing attitude was: "We're all in this together."

The plants in Erie, Somersworth and Louisville are businesses that are going to stay in town, provide jobs and make a profit. That is my kind of high tech.

The Manufacturing Cell
M. William Grant

At Ingersoll-Rand we used the same blueprint for manufacturing for a hundred years. Other companies did

manufacturing. We put machines in a department—the the same. The blueprints were based on functional mill department, the drill department, the grind department. We had conventional, flexible machine tools. And when we needed capacity, we added to the plant or we built a new plant.

This 100-year-old blueprint is still going to be used in some of our operations, but a new blueprint is taking over. It is based on cell manufacturing—others call it group technology, or flow manufacture, or focused manufacture, or family-of-parts manufacture. By my definition, a cell basically takes material and, without putting it back into storage, completes all the tasks to finish the part.

A simple cell is a CNC machine center that can take a casting and complete all the necessary operations. More complex cells require several machine tools. A flexible machining center is a very sophisticated cell.

Ingersoll-Rand was a pioneer in flexible machining, having had a line in our Roanoke, Virginia, plant since 1970. We have had simple cells for many years, and even flexible transfer lines since the early 1960's. These operations, however, have been only islands of progress, and until recently we have never backed them up with a blueprint for a fully integrated manufacturing approach.

The Principles

The important principles of a manufacturing cell are not yet fully achievable, and maybe they never will be. If, however, the project team developing the cell is well grounded in the principles, it will come closer to perfection initially, and will understand and make accommodation for the future development of the cell, which never stops developing.

The first principle is 100-percent quality, not high quality—100 percent quality. By this I mean that the cell cannot produce a bad part, and no inspection is required beyond the cell. Techniques in process gauging with continual feedback capabilities, probes, automatic tool replacement, and automatic post-gauging are available and can be used now.

The second principle is zero setup. The techniques here are provided in the design of machine tools. Today's machine tool offers great capabilities, particularly in the tooling aspects of setup—capabilities such as automatic tool replacement, probes for wear and breakage, ingenious tooling for material handling and loading.

The third principle is to approach unmanned operations. This principle can be implemented with the use of current machine-tool capabilities, including the computer, robotics and built-in material-handling devices supplied by both the machine-tool manufacturer and by devices created in-house from ideas of workers on the factory floor. Those workers have some of the best ideas. A person who has run a chucking machine for 20 years can readily explain how to load a chucking machine automatically.

Zero work-in-process inventory is the fourth principle. Once the principles for quality, set-up and manning have been put in place, lead times for work in process can be substantially lowered. Of course, it is necessary to work with vendors on forecasting and scheduling delivery of required materials to the cell.

Lower lot sizes is the fifth principle. I never thought that I would be preaching to industrial engineers that the best way to lower cost is to decrease quantity. That violates everything I was ever taught, but that is the way to do it now. Through application of the zero setup and the zero work-in-process principles, the actual lot size can be lowered, contributing to better control of inventory and better customer service.

Sixth is zero material handling. The principle of unmanned operations permits automation of loading and movement of material. Or course, the adroit placing of machinery, tools and equipment contributes in large measure to reducing the need for material handling, because the work in process is not stored and moved between functional machining departments.

The seventh principle is one operation, meaning the production of complete parts from the cell. This produces tactical operations improvements, since the scheduling process, the setting of standards, cost accounting, incentive-payment programs, and many other tasks are simplified.

The principle of one operation may be the most important of all. We have been using computers in business for 25 years. That has enabled us rapidly to handle transactions and information flow. The number and complexity of present-day transactions could never have been coped with manually. But we have walked into a trap; we have ignored the importance of reducing transactions and of limiting information flow to significant information. It will not serve us successfully to implement the technology of the factory of the future only to price ourselves out of the marketplace because of the cost of overhead transactions and information flow. The manufacturing cell, with its one-operation approach, allows for significant improvements in this area, and we must achieve them—perhaps in the face of opposition from financial managers.

Employee management is the last principle. All employees within the cell should be trained to perform all operations required, both horizontally and vertically, to run all the machine tools. Further they should contribute to equipment design and material handling systems and programming. Each one should have a sense of responsibility for the cell's success.

Results

What happens if we adopt and follow these principles?

Here are some results of their partial application in a 450,000 square-foot Ingersoll-Rand tool plant in Athens, Pennsylvania.

—Travel of material flowing through the plant was reduced by 80 percent, from something over a mile to a few hundred yards.

—Floor space was reduced by 50 percent.

—The number of production steps was reduced by 50 percent.

—Set-up time was reduced by 75 percent.

—Lead time was reduced by 83 percent, from forty-two days to seven days. (Seven days is probably too long. Two days ought to be the norm, but we can only push so far so fast.)

—Quality is approaching 100 percent.

What has helped us immeasurably in achieving these gains is the attitude of the people on the manufacturing floor. They have been well disposed to participate in, to contribute to the factory of the future. The challenge for every management is to bring the technical capabilities and the human capabilities together.

Reorganizing and Retooling to Capture a Larger Market Share
Hayward Thomas

Ten years ago, Broan Manufacturing Company was a small, privately owned ventilating equipment manufacturer—one of many in an industry dominated by NuTone and Burns Air King. The president was determined to become a dominant factor in the industry. He put together a talented team of engineers, finance, human-resources, manufacturing and marketing people. He himself was a strong contributor in the product-development and marketing areas. His philosophy was to invest capital in first-class facilities, systems, tools and equipment, providing capacity far beyond our immediate needs. (More details about those investments below.)

As a result of these steps, Broan is now the dominant supplier in the kitchen range-hood sector of the industry and a very important factor in supplying the overall home-ventilation market. Some of the significant events in this transition were:

—In 1970, Broan began installation of an MRP system which was partly developed in-house, and which was, for its time, at the leading edge of the technology.

—In 1972, Broan purchased the "Nautilus" kitchen range-hood business from one of the major white goods companies. This gave us entry to the retail and original equipment manufacturer (OEM) markets with a product of substantially different design and appearance. We could sell hoods broadly without disrupting our basic housing-oriented business.

—During the 1974 and 1975 housing recession, Broan continued to merchandise and market aggressively, and as a result was able to pick up sufficient market share to maintain sales levels.

—Throughout this period, the president focused the efforts of the entire organization on becoming the dominant manufacturer in our industry. A strategic planning process was developed and a five year plan implemented. As an outgrowth of this planning process, major building additions were put in place in 1974 and 1977, well ahead of the actual need for additional capacity.

—In 1975, we earned the custom range-hood business of one of the country's leading mass merchandisers, and immediately began a campaign to obtain all that company's hood business.

—Extensive studies of the market and the programs and offerings of our competitors were undertaken and integrated with information from our field sales force. From this effort it became clear that the needs of the mainstream volume kitchen range-hood market could be served with three basic models.

We began planning to move in this direction. This planning accelerated in the latter part of 1976, when it became apparent that we had an excellent opportunity to become the major supplier to the mass merchandiser already mentioned.

Redesigning and Retooling

Performance specifications, cost targets, and required features were determined. The opinion was confirmed that if we were to achieve our objective of dominating the industry, Broan could not simply tool the product for the new customer in the usual way and continue with a multiplicity of models. Instead, we would make a major investment in completely redesigning and retooling the total kitchen range-hood line, integrating product design with process, tooling and equipment design. This was a systems approach for maximum productivity and minimum product cost.

The conceptualization of the product design and the manufacturing process had gone hand in glove with the marketing studies and the development of the product specifications. We had put aside all of our preconceived engineering and manufacturing notions of how a range hood should be designed and manufactured. We called in equipment suppliers, looked at fully automated lines, evaluated plastic construction, and considered many alternatives before the combined marketing, engineering, manufacturing and finance team settled on the product design and manufacturing system approach that was to be followed.

The technical challenge to the product-engineering and manufacturing part of the organization was to develop designs, equipment and facilities that would:

(1) Permit the manufacture of large volumes of standardized product at low cost;
(2) Permit product appearance differentiation;
(3) Be responsive to the lumpy demand experienced in our business, that is, permit shifting production from one model or one customer to another on very short notice.

The top manufacturing and engineering executives spent many hours together planning the design and equipment that would meet these challenges. Since standardizing the product was essential to success, three basic models were designed.

Organization

Did we have to reorganize to capture a larger market share? No, not in the sense of changing the lines or boxes on our organization chart. What we did, and what is the essence of the matter, was to get swept up in an enthusiastic team effort in which the parochial and territorial evils of functionalism were almost completely eliminated.

In my experience, one does not need to change the organizational structure in a medium-sized company, like Broan, to get the desired results. Even in some large companies, the organization chart is not the key. Having the right leadership at a high enough level to bring the functions together is an absolute requirement for superior performance in planning and carrying out a major retooling effort or, for that matter, in carrying out any significant program that crosses functional lines. Certainly, organizational structures that promote interfunctional teamwork are to be favored. However, almost any organizational structure will work well with the right leadership, and almost any can fall apart without it. After all is said and done, someone at the top, or very close to it, has to understand what is needed and then, with strong determination, take whatever steps are necessary to make it happen. Any major project involving new technology must include:

• Sound planning, based on intimate knowledge of markets and products;
• Close interfunctional teamwork; and
• Top management's willingness to commit capital and human resources to achieve long-term results.

We believe these are essential ingredients to increasing productivity and maintaining technological leadership. The Broan experience demonstrates that they work.

Manufacturing Objectives and Strategies
Thomas L. Skelly[1]

The manufacturing objectives of the Xerox Memorywriter Program included the support of market demand on a worldwide basis. The product quality had to be second to none and, therefore, we established quality programs at both the suppliers (see below) and the Office Products Division to *drive* the quality process and control from the *piece* parts *basis upward* to finished goods. We had to establish an intensive product cost-reduction effort from the start of the design cycle, and plan to continue that effort through the entire product life by the use of value analysis and value-engineering teams, early supplier involvement, employee involvement programs, and assembly automation. In order to control overhead and improve asset management, we had to reduce historic production inventory levels while increasing the volume of output. We established a target for automating the procurement and material-planning processes so that we could easily adjust our suppliers' planned deliveries, schedules and material-receipt planning. This would provide a minimum of problems associated with configuration control and design change cut-in planning. And, lastly, we wanted to automate the material flow through the manufacturing facility so that we knew what material was available and where it was needed, and could provide it at the point of use with minimum intervention.

In order to accomplish the manufacturing objectives, the following manufacturing strategy was put in place. A highly automated production facility would be a requirement. The development of a computer-controlled material handling and inventory-management system would be designed on a systems basis from the receiving dock to the shipping dock. One month of supply of inventory was set as the asset management target. The manufacturing process should produce the lowest possible product cost to maintain our competitive edge in the marketplace. Less than one hour of assembly time would be required for each typewriter. This was a design target as well as a manufacturing strategy. The computer-controlled system would be tied in with the order-entry system, and provide the capability to ship directly to the customer from the end of the production line. The manufacturing strategy had to take into account capacity growth on a worldwide basis. Therefore, we had to evaluate multiple manufacturing locations in the United States, Europe, Canada, Latin America, and Japan, and develop a process for controlling quality, configuration and design change cut-ins. The design of the manufacturing process was accomplished in parallel with the Memorywriter product design and a closely coordinated effort between development, marketing and manufacturing had to be maintained to meet overall objectives.

In 1982, the acceptance of the Memorywriter product was outstanding and we are on target with respect to sales, new product introductions, product cost, and overall quality and reliability.

Ensuring Quality from Suppliers

At the outset we did have problems with suppliers' product quality. This was due in part to our own perception of what was acceptable. If you indicate to someone (not necessarily in words) that you will accept a certain quality level, if you show them that you will accept a lower quality level either by providing safety stock or by setting up processes to send material back easily or to hold the material, you are not going to get the quality levels that you need from the suppliers.

But you can say: "I am not going to have safety stock in my place because of process-control problems in your place. If safety stock is needed, then you are going to absorb that cost." The only reason for having safety stock, after all, is because there is a supplier process problem or a supplier delivery problem. And whose fault is that? Unless there is a design shortcoming in the product, it is the suppliers' responsibility to deliver a quality product.

We made sure that quality control systems were in place in our suppliers and that they understood we wanted 100 percent quality. When 100 percent quality was not available, they had two options: to bail out of the program, which is not what we wanted them to do, or to make safety stock available at their own cost either at their locations or at our Dallas plant so it would not shut down because of the suppliers' quality problems.

I think that this posture really gets the suppliers' attention because they are picking up part of the cost that the user used to pick up. This, in turn, stimulates the suppliers to solve their quality problems, and to work closely with the user to determine what is acceptable.

[1]Mr. Skelly was Vice President of Manufacturing, Office Products Division, Xerox Corporation, when he made the presentation on which this paper is based at the conference on "Meeting the New Industrial Competition."

Part V

Human Resources and the New Technology

Manufacturing, Today and Tomorrow:
The Work Force and Company Infrastructure
Erich Bloch

U.S. industry is undergoing massive change, change that has its origins in the technological innovations of the last 25 years, especially computers, semiconductors, and automation with robotics. Although the United States has been in the forefront of these developments, we have not been first or unchallenged in their exploitation in recent years.

First, a brief glance at some larger problems or trends that affect manufacturing: One is world competition. Trade patterns are now truly international. This development has been caused primarily by the quick and wide diffusion of technology, which, in turn, has led to increased competition. For many nations, being leaders in new technologies is a national imperative, and one sees examples of government-industry collaboration to this end.

We suffer from institutional obsolescence in the United States. This is true in industry and in academia; it is probably also true in government. One way for industry to renew itself is to practice participative management instead of traditional authoritative management. There are encouraging signs that industry will do so.

We need to focus on long-term strategy instead of short-term profit, a lesson that we are learning, albeit very slowly. More generally, the classical rules of management are now meaningless. We are finding new ones. The ratio of indirect cost to direct cost is changing so rapidly that it is approaching infinity. In the past, three-to-one or two-to-one ratios were deemed acceptable, even optimal. People have to change with the rules. We need more and different training.

Another significant development is the structural change in industry. By all measurements and observations, employment in the industrial sector is declining, that in the information and service sector is increasing. Professor James Brian Quinn estimates that by 1990 the services and information sector will account for 75 percent of employment in the United States. Manufacturing will have dropped to 18 percent; agriculture and mining to about 3 percent. These will be vast changes (considering that in 1960 the manufacturing sector was 30 percent and the services and information sector was 50 percent of total employment), with accompanying dislocation both on the personal and on a corporate level. This does not mean that the manufacturing sector will be less important than it has been in the past. In absolute numbers, this sector probably will employ more people than it did ten years ago, or even now.

Manufacturing Issues

In manufacturing, the loss of our leading edge, lack of focus, inadequate quality, and poor productivity are all troublesome. Although our absolute productivity is still higher than any other country's, Japan and West Germany, among others, are closing the gap very rapidly. U.S. plants are older, on average, than those of our trading partners: Sixteen years as against nine or ten years. And the reason is obvious: Our capital investment is consistently lower than that of Japan and West Germany. It is well-known that capital investment and manufacturing productivity are closely tied together.

It is also a fact that productivity is really governed, to a first-order effect, by technological innovation. That is not only true in development and research; it is equally true in manufacturing. To use my own industry as an example: The cost of computing has decreased by two orders of magnitude in 30 years, during which period there was a fourfold increase in the consumer price index.

This decrease would not have been possible if it had not been for constant innovation in technology and the incorporation of this innovation into products.

In no area has U.S. industry's inattention been more damaging than in quality. One reason there is a demand for higher quality is that the application of new technology requires it. Beyond that, the consumer is more quality conscious than in the past, primarily because of inflation and unemployment. There is a disparity of views about quality that I think should give us concern. In 1982, the Professional Society of Quality Engineers queried some CEO's and some consumers about quality. The first question was: How has quality of U.S.-made products changed? Ninety percent of the CEO's replied that it is "better than," or "equal to," what it was in the past. Seventy-five percent of the consumers chose "worse than" or "equal to" answers. The second question was: How does the quality of U.S. products compare with the quality of foreign products? Seventy-eight percent of the CEO's gave U.S. products a "better" or "equal" ranking; seventy-five percent of the consumers rated U.S. products "worse" or "equal." Who is right? The consumer, obviously.

Reduced R&D spending is another pertinent issue. R&D expenditure as a percent of GNP decreased from close to 3 percent to about 2.3 percent between 1970 and 1980. It is again on the upswing, one hopes at a very rapid rate. But, in recent years, the ratios in other countries—Japan, West Germany, and France in particular—have been increasing considerably.

It is true that we are still spending more on R&D in absolute terms than any of our trading partners, indeed, more than many of our trading partners combined. But consider that much U.S. spending on R&D is defense-related, and does not always benefit the industrial and consumer sectors. Further, foreign R&D, especially Japanese R&D, is concentrated on target areas—semiconductors, computers, pharmaceuticals, consumer electronics; R&D is more dispersed in the United States. As a consequence, U.S. spending in absolute sums in specific industry sectors is not much different from other countries' spending. This is certainly true for the semiconductor industry.

We now hear a lot about the crisis in engineering. There is a very real shortage of engineering school faculty: Some 10 percent of engineering faculty positions are vacant nationwide, as a result of the declining numbers of U.S. doctoral candidates and the decreased attractiveness of academic careers as compared with careers in industry. One result of this faculty shortage could be a chronic shortage of engineers for years to come. But, in my opinion, the real problem is not so much a matter of numbers as of quality and the appropriateness of skills. Each year, Japan, with half our population, produces more electrical engineering graduates than we do. What happens to all these Japanese graduates? For one thing, a higher proportion is employed in manufacturing than in the United States. While employment of scientists and engineers has been increasing in the private sector, their number in manufacturing has been decreasing. This is a legacy, I think, of the view that manufacturing is secondary to research and development. It is not just the view of industry but of the universities as well. The best and the brightest did not go into manufacturing in the past, but we must attract them if we want to succeed in the future.

Changes in Manufacturing

Profound changes are occurring in manufacturing. The Industrial Revolution of the 19th century was brought about by the exploitation of energy, leading to the consolidation of manufacturing resources and their organization into activities capitalizing on economy of scale. Labor was the focal point. In this century, and especially since World War II, we have seen the automation of individual tools and the drive for better and automated procedures for logistics and control. The focus has been primarily, if not completely, on hard technology.

What we see on the horizon is the development of the necessary technology to proceed in a significant way to the next step, namely, the total integration of the manufacturing process, including design. (Design is part of the manufacturing process, and we had better learn that soon.) One can discern this trend in the changing ratio of indirect to direct costs, mentioned earlier. Therefore, we need to change our model of manufacturing. The new model should depict manufacturing as two parallel but related activities: (1) the hardware, or highly automated physical plant that makes the product; and (2) the software—the design, the organization, the scheduling, the control of the process, the feedback into the process, the feed-forward from the process, a series of automated data-processing operations.

I would guess that the greatest barrier to decisions to automate or to accept this new systems approach to manufacturing is the fear of being unable to accommodate to changed circumstances quickly and without loss of capital. That argues that we must take the long-term view, and that we be willing to take strategic risks.

Most present-day computerized factory systems consist of unconnected islands of automation—islands of design, production planning, material handling, assembly, inspection, and so on. The task ahead is to link these islands into integrated systems.

The pursuit of this task will cause changes in the relationship between research and development and manufacturing. The domains are overlapping more; boundaries are more difficult to define. The technical sophistication in manufacturing is increasing and will be on a par with the level of sophistication in research and development, once integrated manufacturing systems are a reality.

Technological disciplines are also changing dramatically. Circuit design is now being done by modeling on a computer rather than by experimentation on a bench. Of course, modeling requires a different approach, and different education for the people doing it.

I would draw these conclusions: Manufacturing is becoming more science and technology based, requiring more and better trained people; and development, design and product engineering are changing in both content and approach, with new tools, new disciplines, new interactions.

CAD/CAM technology is an example. It first penetrated electrical and electronic engineering, especially circuit and logic design, physical implementation like chip layout, and systems simulation. It has now begun to appear in mechanical design, where I believe the penetration will be a lot faster than it was in the electrical and electronic areas because many of the same approaches are applicable there.

The effect of computer-aided approaches on productivity in the design function itself is very great. Sometimes a thirtyfold improvement has resulted; more commonly, there is a fivefold gain. But these systems are never finished. They need regularly to incorporate newer advances, newer approaches, newer technologies.

What Has To Be Done

What is necessary to get on top of the situation; to recapture the manufacturing lead? Three things are needed. The first is to adopt a systems approach to automation, which I have discussed. The second and third go together: efficient and effective use of the work force, and education to remedy the shortage of critical skills or to retrain people lacking these skills.

The new manufacturing environment requires a well-trained work force that is well motivated and that accepts new developments and new technologies. The work force must be part of the decision process, and must be given the opportunity to be trained in the new approaches, tools and procedures before the new machine or robot is wheeled into the plant.

How fast a company automates is not necessarily a question of available technology, but the acceptance of the new approach and resulting environment by the total organization. I think that middle management is probably more a laggard in this regard than any other group in a company.

We also have to find out if we have an adequate supply of manufacturing engineers and manufacturing personnel who can work in this new environment; who know

automation and how to manage quality and why things work. These people require a broad range of skills, quite distinct from, yet linked to product-innovation skills. We are no longer interested in the classical industrial engineer. We are interested in the systems engineer who is versed in management and in the relevant technologies.

In the Fall of 1982, IBM announced an initiative to support academe in the development of a graduate-level curriculum in manufacturing-systems engineering. What led to this initiative was our belief that the state of manufacturing today is not what it should be, and that the changes in manufacturing that I have been discussing make this a subject worthy of academic research and teaching. IBM announced that it would spend $50 million for equipment and for curriculum development to this end. The response has been gratifying. Only a small number of the 140 universities that have applied will benefit from this program, but its indirect benefits as a model for support from other industry sources should be considerable.

But industry also needs to turn inward to its own technical people and its own human resources in general, and bring them up to date with changing technical requirements. The rate of obsolescence of knowledge is accelerating. The cost to support a professional is increasing not only in salary, but in tools, equipment, work stations, and communications networks. Lifelong, continuing education is required and deserves increased attention from industry as well as academe.

At IBM we have a program for sending people to get Ph.D. degrees in disciplines that are important to the knowledge base of IBM laboratories and research organizations. Formerly we paid program participants 75 percent of their regular salaries. We have increased this to 100 percent. It has been a very small program, involving 15 to 20 people per year. We are looking at ways to increase it, but it will never grow to the point of 100 participants a year. I think it is more important to be selective—in the people chosen and in the subject matter—than to have a large program.

More important is our decentralized continuing education activity, which attracts about 1,500 people yearly. The end-product usually is a master's degree. It used to take a long time to gain a degree in this program. We have changed that of late by allowing a participant, upon accumulation of half the credits for the degree, to enroll in a university for one semester of full-time study at full pay to complete the degree requirements.

A third company effort is a directive that requires that every technical professional and technical manager devote 40 hours each year to technical education or training sponsored by IBM, universities or professional societies.

Two years ago we founded a Manufacturing Technology Institute to improve the productivity of the manufacturing engineer and the design engineer. There we are training manufacturing people who, having been out of school for five to fifteen years, have not been exposed to some of the new technologies and the new approaches. It is a full-time, ten-week course. Here, too, selection is the key; the selection process is very vigorously controlled from a quality viewpoint. We are trying to attract the best people for this activity.

The ten-week program includes elective courses as well as core curriculum. They are taught at approximately the master's degree level. Many of the courses are taught by university professors associated with IBM, as well as by people from within IBM. There is always homework associated with the courses; the examples studied are real examples out of the IBM experience. Some of the practical solutions worked out in the courses are being fed back to the manufacturing organizations and to the development organizations that had the problems in the first place.

Some Fundamental Propositions

Manufacturing is changing to an integrated systems approach. It is driven by innovation and new technologies, which, in turn, cause significant changes in the professional disciplines and the education and training of all employees. And a different management approach is required to manage in this new world with these new technologies.

The nation and U.S. industry have important assets: An educable work force; natural and financial resources; a new spirit of cooperation between industry and academe, and even between government and industry, with much more government understanding of industry's problems; some movement on the question of opening trade with some of the countries that have erected barriers. All of these signs and developments should make us optimistic about the future of U.S. industry.

The Westinghouse Program
Thomas J. Murrin

When we began our quality and productivity efforts in 1979, we were not planning to transform the management style of the corporation. Rather, we wanted to improve our performance, particularly in customer service and in operating profitability. Operating margins were not satisfactory and Westinghouse was becoming concerned about increasing worldwide competition.

We formed a corporate committee on productivity, which I chaired, and began an extensive study in the United States, Europe and the Pacific Basin with eventual emphasis on Japan. These studies alerted us to

the critical linkage between productivity and quality, and to the awesome concentration on manufacturing technology and the devotion to quality of many of our foreign competitors. These studies convinced top management that substantial changes were needed.

Accordingly, Westinghouse launched a major campaign to improve quality and productivity—and began implementing significant changes throughout the corporation to achieve these objectives. A Vice President of Corporate Quality and Productivity was appointed and, subsequently, a Productivity and Quality Center was established apparently the first such initiatives in the United States. About 300 full-time employees are now assigned to the Center, working on quality and productivity programs throughout the corporation.

Do it Right the First Time

We have expedited the introduction of improved technology to let us do the job right the first time with the right tools. Many of our efforts to apply new technology are aimed at making our white-collar workers more productive, because they constitute over half our work force. The availability of a myriad of new, powerful hardware and software systems—including not only CAD, CAM, CAT, and interactive graphics, but also electronic mail, voice switching, word processing, high-speed facsimile transmission and printing, and teleconferencing—makes this a most exciting and promising area.

We now see that "doing it right the first time" has an immense potential for improved productivity, customer satisfaction, international competitiveness, and, ultimately, improved profitability. For example, considerable cash and profits can be generated by reducing failure costs. It is only when we really manage for quality that we become aware of the hidden costs of failure: Costs that management often does not consider, but that reduce profitability with devastating effects.

One particularly significant statistic from several years of data analysis confirms a multiplier effect between the cost of failure and profit margins. Although the specific effect differs from product to product, a conservative estimate is four-to-one: That is, for each $1 reduction in failure costs, we add about $4 to profit margin.

Spreading the Word

To cultivate the total quality attitude throughout the organization, every Westinghouse management meeting for the last four years has had the theme of quality and productivity, and every list of annual key objectives begins with quality and productivity-improvement goals. To reinforce this theme, we have improved our communications programs. Videotape is the communications tool that is most effective for us. Seeing and hearing a message, particularly when it comes over a television screen, is a more powerful and persuasive communciations method than anything we have used in the past. Accordingly, we have created a corporatewide videotape program to encourage quality and productivity-improvement attitudes and methods.

We also have under way an in-house training program on the statistical design of experiments and other modern statistics methodologies. We believe that it is crucial for the improvement of product quality and process efficiency that management and professional people learn powerful statistical methods, particularly the statistical design of experiments. This is one opportunity that may enable us to leapfrog the Japanese. The hand-held calculator makes possible effective on-the-factory-floor use of many statistical methods once left only to statistical experts.

We have also placed a major emphasis on working with Westinghouse's key suppliers to make them part of the team. For example, the people in our Defense Center, in Baltimore, have their vendors participate in the design and specification process, and in assessing the manufacturability of our products. (For details of another program to enhance the quality of suppliers' products, see page 39.)

We have created a Quality Seed Fund to provide the wherewithal for high-risk, high-promise initiatives. An excellent example of a quality-improvement initiative is the printed wiring assembly program at the Defense Center. Two years ago, we made a commitment to decrease the amount of rework required on sophisticated wiring assemblies, and a detailed plan was developed to address all of the proven detractors. To our dismay, we found that only about 12 percent of our assemblies were making it all the way through the process successfully the first time. In 1982, the "first-time-through" figure was over 60 percent; in 1983, it is over 80 percent; and we are confident of reaching about 95 percent by the end of 1985. Productivity is up dramatically—as are employee morale and customer satisfaction.

Involving People

It is necessary for industry to improve the motivation and the management of people, with emphasis on getting them involved in the identification and solution of problems through a participative management approach. Quality circles are, perhaps, the simplest way we, at Westinghouse, have to involve our people more effectively. We now have about 2,000 quality circles at over 200 locations. Although we found the quality-circle concept in Japan, we believe it has been extended by applying it to white-collar, as well as blue-collar, employees. In all, over 18,000 Westinghouse employees are involved in quality circles, and this number increases by several hundred each month.

Participative management has already had a dramatic impact. By challenging their intelligence and appealing to their innate sense of quality, we find that people are taking new pride in their work, and are developing a personal stake in quality, reliability and productivity. At one division, the hourly employees, encouraged to assume more responsibility for product quality, asked for and received authorization to stop production when quality standards are not being met. They know that their supervisors not only will support such action, but also resolve the problems in a constructive way. This not only involves responsibility for one's own work, but also an awareness of overall product requirements flowing through the work areas. (For another company's experience with participative management, see page 45.)

Westinghouse is also providing increased training opportunities. Many employees throughout U.S. industry are becoming victims of "technology shock." This is especially true of older engineers. By present-day standards, much of what they learned in school is obsolete. Therefore, we have instituted programs designed to reeducate veteran engineers in many of our high-technology organizations. And (through the shared-growth program) we are providing tuition-assisted advanced educational opportunities for technicians and nonprofessional employees.

We are also conducting quality seminars for executive management to acquaint senior executives with how they can become visibly and effectively involved in quality improvement. For example, they can ensure that key quality issues and actions are included in each business unit's strategic plan, and can allocate necessary resources to support quality-enhancement activities. And they can make quality improvement an important element of each subordinate's performance appraisal.

Over the long term, the education and training of our people may be the most important element in a continuous total quality improvement concept. For without a properly trained, educated and committed work force, U.S. industry simply will not be able to compete effectively in the world marketplace. Happily, at Westinghouse we find that almost all our people have a strong desire to contribute to quality improvement—and greatly enjoy the recognition that they get for their contributions.

We in industry must think even more open-mindedly and creatively about how we can increase the qualitative strength of our work force. And we need to formulate a more effective alliance with educational institutions to improve technical training, and to satisfy the serious shortage of critical scientific and vocational skills.

Worker Motivation and Participative Management
M. William Grant

The factory floor is changing more rapidly than ever before, and the challenge the factory floor represents is more important than it has ever been. Consider, for example, the worker-motivation aspect of process automation. There are many phrases to describe what is happening in this field: participative management, quality circles, quality of work life, productivity programs. These efforts are contributing on the factory floor to real productivity gains and to profits.

The historic relationships between supervisors and those supervised is changing. Ideas and implementation of them are coming from a wide spectrum of employees. What is happening to the authoritative style management is about what happened to the slide rule when calculators arrived.

Evidence of these changes is apparent in Ingersoll-Rand's factories. In a program at one bearings plant, employees have established their own production norms. Every two hours, they get feedback from the supervisor against these norms; and they get help rather than hell if they are below par. This approach is saving over $1 million a year. Other plants now are using the same approach; in fact, in our newest plant, the supervisors have been eliminated as an experiment. We believe that more of our employees are now just as interested as management in company performance, and realize that profitability is the key to job security and their future.

Another evidence of this concern of employees is in our union plants, where we see a demand on the part of employees to participate in decisions. When union policy or union management obstructs this desire, the employees eventually decertify the union. We have had nine plants, some large, some small, decertified over the last three or four years.

The Changing Role of Middle Management
H.E. Bovay, Jr.

Many pieces of the factory of the future are distributed throughout the entire infrastructure of most organizations, and are not just from on the factory floor. From my vantage point, I can see technological changes ahead that will provide new and increased managerial challenges and objectives for top management.

As for the other people who may be involved in the restructuring of U.S. industry, I believe we can expect a new breed of middle managers. The recession has caused the streamlining of most industrial organizations. As a result of scientific innovation, middle managers need no longer be information processors for top executives, who now have direct access to the same data. In my opinion, the analysis and preparation of data by middle management will simply no longer be needed as electronic hardware invades the executive office.

The new breed of middle managers will have more technical appreciation, and will be more capable than their predecessors of taking charge of larger parts of an organization. And they will be looking abroad and becoming involved in global joint ventures and technological developments with the leaders of other countries' industries. Some examples of this breed are now appearing on the scene.

Part VI
A Summing Up

Improving Industrial Competitiveness
Robert J. Allio

Various remedies for the problems of competition have been propounded by the contributors to this report. All have merit, but taken individually, none will suffice as a prescription to business managers in the current difficult competitive environment. Managers must adopt a broad approach; indeed, a reductionist approach to survival may be fatal.

The task of survival, renewal and growth requires a corporate response to three superordinate issues:

(1) The *global strategies* enacted by key competitors in many industries.

(2) The opportunity and challenge presented by *new technologies.*

(3) The comparative advantage displayed by firms that have *quality management.*

Global Strategies

The regional or national strategy is no longer appropriate for many industries. The list of global industries is expanding at a rapid pace. It includes not only industrial products such as steel and oil, but also consumer products such as automobiles, motorcycles, television sets, beverages and cosmetics. The hegemony of the U.S. firm has waned in the face of vigorous competition from firms that have adopted global strategies.

A more anticipatory approach to globalization is needed. For example, progressive managers will seek early opportunities to develop and carry out a global strategy. Leading indicators include the emergence of common customer needs (cola drinks), standardization of components (semiconductors), and the establishment of global quality standards (photographic film, audiotape and videotape).

The elements of a global approach to competition include an environmental scanning process and a global information system (e.g., for market-share calculation). In addition, the organizational form must emphasize product or service focus, as opposed to the market focus found in national or regional industries.

Technology

Technology will be a key success factor in most industries of the 1980's. Managers need to apply the benefits of technology in two situations:

• *Innovation.* The vitality of an economic system suffering from maturity and decline in many of its industries is strongly dependent on a continuing flow of new ventures. The key to leadership in embryonic industries is almost invariably technology.

• *Productivity.* In a mature industry, the primary basis of competition shifts away from product features and function to cost and price. Technology can then be invoked to improve efficiency and productivity. It is in this latter domain that we find the application of automation and more effective factory design yielding maximum benefits.

Managers in high-technology industries allocate resources to the development of technology-based products and services. In low-technology industries, on the other hand, technology must be applied to reduce cost, improve productivity, and add value to the product. New technology thus can be used either to add value to the product or to reduce cost and price. In every industry, therefore, be it high or low technology, managers will need to administer the technological resources of their corporation more effectively and apply technology to the solution of management problems.

Managerial Quality

The major opportunities to improve organizational productivity derive only in part from greater automation of manufacturing or higher output per worker. Improvements in managerial productivity represent an even greater opportunity. How can managers be more productive? Two principal factors need to be considered:

• *Management selection.* Corporations are notorious for their thoughtless allocation of managers to tasks within the organization. A typical example is the assignment of a new venture responsibility to the most experienced executive, regardless of whether that manager has relevant experience, or even any entrepreneurial spirit. The evidence is mounting that assigning managers to strategies for which they are suited by experience, skill or temperament can make an important difference in organizational performance.

Linking reward systems to desired performance represents still another opportunity to improve managerial productivity.

• *Management education.* The renewal of our organizations by technological innovation must be accompanied by an equal commitment to managerial reeducation. New or expanded managerial responsibilities demand new skills, viewpoints and techniques. Changing environments and tougher competition usually demand new strategies (and the ability to think strategically). And new management technology emerges continually—a manager is handicapped if he is not acquainted with new methods for marketing, economic modeling, and inventory control, for example.

We may underestimate the pervasive and systemic nature of our declining competitive strength. Regaining leadership will require an examination of all the many options available for recovery.

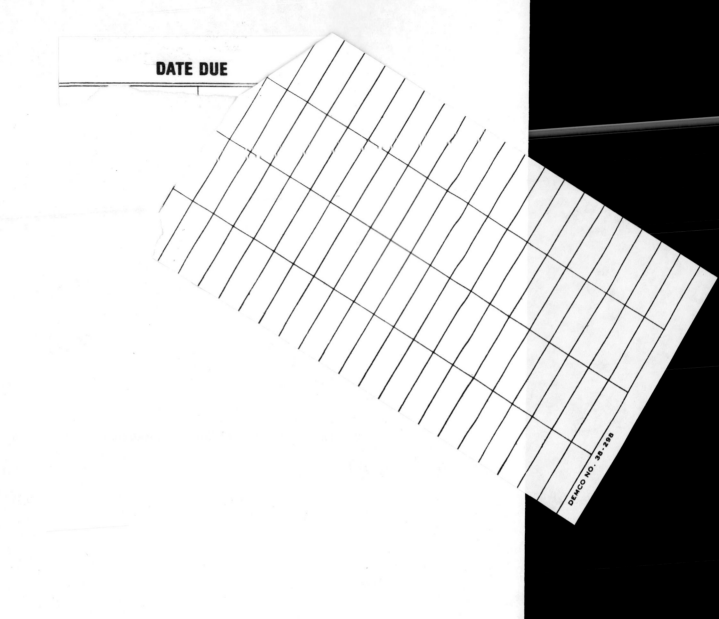

DATE DUE